JUST ENOUGH GERMAN

Just Enough German

Christine Bunnenberg-Waterman

Hugo's Language Books Limited

© 1994 Hugo's Language Books Ltd
All rights reserved
ISBN 0 85285 222 3

'Just Enough German' is also available in a pack with two
cassettes, ISBN 0 85285 223 1

Written by
Christine Bunnenberg-Waterman

Edited by
Ruth Nason

Set in Palatino and Optima by
Andrew Burrell

Printed and bound in Great Britain by
Scotprint

Contents

Preface

You may be planning a trip to Germany, either for a holiday or on business. If so, your visit will be all the more enjoyable if you are able to understand the language you hear about you, and can have a go at communicating in German yourself.

Some first German courses are so simple that you end up knowing only how to ask some of the most obvious tourists' questions. You find they have taught you too little. Others try to teach you too much and frighten you off with all the formal rules they set out. This course aims to give you "Just Enough" – enough knowledge and enough confidence to enjoy some real German conversation.

The first chapter explains how German is pronounced, and also gives you practice with numbers and dates.

The following seven chapters each revolve around an aspect of German everyday life and at the same time introduce you, progressively, to important language points and vocabulary.

Each chapter opens with a set of dialogues – which you can also listen to on the **Just Enough German** tapes, if you have these as well. Have fun listening to the sections called "How it sounds!" One follows each dialogue. Next you will find some useful Information about modern German customs, some clear Language Notes, and a Word List of all the new vocabulary introduced in the chapter.

Also in each chapter you will find some exercises to help you practise the language points and vocabulary – the answers are at the end of the chapter! Some of the exercises involve working with the tapes, which we feel make **Just Enough German** even more enjoyable to follow.

Viel Glück und Prost auf Ihr Deutsch!

1 Practise Pronouncing!

Luckily, German pronunciation is quite easy for English speakers. There are just a few essential rules to learn, if you want to pronounce words correctly. Good pronunciation will guarantee that people understand what you are saying, so it is well worth putting in some effort to learn the rules and practise pronouncing!

If you can, use the tapes which go with this book. The tape symbol indicates that you will find something on tape to help you practise.

THE ALPHABET

It's a good idea to learn how the alphabet sounds in German. You may be asked to spell your name, for instance, when you make a reservation at a hotel or restaurant.

A	ah	H	hah	O	oh	V	fow
B	bay	I	ee	P	pay	W	vay
C	tsay	J	yott	Q	koo	X	iks
D	day	K	kah	R	airr	Y	ip-see-lon
E	ay	L	ell	S	ess	Z	tset
F	eff	M	emm	T	tay		
G	gay	N	enn	U	oo		

Special German characters: Ä Ö Ü ß

If you can, listen to the alphabet on the tape and repeat after each letter. When you listen again, underline the letters you find difficult to pronounce. Listen as often as you like, until you feel really confident.

Now let's look at how the letters sound in the context of some basic German words.

VOWELS: A,E,I,O,U,Y

Do you find the vowels most difficult to pronounce? Sometimes a vowel is "short" and sometimes it is "long". It depends on the word in which it appears. A vowel is always long when it is followed by "h", and also when it is followed by a single consonant only. A vowel is short when it is followed by more than one consonant. Practise saying the following:

a	Mann (*man*)	short, almost as in the English "*cut*"
	Abend (*evening*)	long, as in the English "*bar*"
e	Bett (*bed*)	short, as in "*get*"
	nehmen (*to take*)	long, as in "*lane*"
i	ist (*is*)	short, as in "*fit*"
	Ihr (*your*)	long, as in "*near*"
o	Stop (*stop*)	short, as in "*pot*"
	wohnen (to live)	long, as in "*home*"
u	Kuß (*kiss*)	short, as in "*book*"
	gut (*good*)	long, as in "*fool*"
y	Mythe (*myth*)	short "u" sound, as in English "*dune*" or French "*une*"

VOWELS WITH UMLAUTS: Ä, Ö, Ü

The two dots over these vowels are called the umlaut. The umlaut changes the sound of the vowels.

ä	Städte (*towns*)	short "e" sound, as in English "*pet*"
	Käse (*cheese*)	long "e" sound, as in English "*air*"
ö	möchte (*would like*)	short "er" sound, as in English "*dirt*" or French "*oeuf*"
	Öl (*oil*)	long "er" sound, as above, but more drawn out
ü	Glück (*luck*)	short "u" sound, as in English "*dune*" or French "*une*"
	süß (*sweet*)	long "u" sound, as above but more drawn out

COMBINED VOWELS (DIPHTHONGS): AI, EI, AU, EU, ÄU

These combinations of vowels are always pronounced as follows:

ai	Mai (*May*)	"i" sound, as in English "*sigh*"
ei	mein (*mine*)	"i" sound, as in English "*sigh*"
au	Frau (*woman*)	"ow" sound, as in English "*now*"
eu	neun (*nine*)	"oy" sound, as in English "*toy*"
äu	Bäume (*trees*)	"oy" sound, as in English "*toy*"

These words are all on the tape for you to practise repeating the sounds, if you can.

CONSONANTS

Many of the consonants are pronounced just as in English. They may sound slightly different if they are at the end of a word. Here are some words for you to practise with. They are all on the **Just Enough German** tape, too.

b	Bett (*bed*)	as in English "*bed*"
	ab (*away*)	"p" sound, as in English "*cup*"
c	hardly exists on its own. It is usually in combination with	"k" or "h"
ck	Blick (*look*)	as in English "*look*"
ch	ich (*I*)	"h", as in "*Hugo*"
	Buch (*book*)	"ch", as in the Scottish pronunciation of "*loch*"
d	du (*you*)	as in English "*dead*"
	Hund (*dog*)	"t" sound, as in English "*want*"
f	fünf (*five*)	as in English "*fit*" and "*tiff*"
g	gut (*good*)	as in English "*go*"
	Tag (*day*)	"ck" sound, as in English "*tack*"
	wichtig (*important*)	"h" sound, as in "*Hugo*"
h	Hand (*hand*)	as in English "*hand*"
j	ja (*yes*)	"y" sound, as in English "*yes*"
k	kaufen (*to buy*)	as in English "*king*"
l	Lied (*song*)	as in English "*lift*"
m	Mutter (*mother*)	as in English "*mother*"
n	nicht (not)	as in English "*not*"
ng	singen (*to sing*)	as in English "*ringing*"
p	Platz (*place*)	as in English "*place*"

11

pf	**Pf**und (*pound*)	the "p" and "f" are pronounced quickly, one after the other
q	**Qu**atsch (*nonsense*)	"kv"
r	**r**ichtig (*correct*)	"r" similar to the Scottish, formed in the back of the throat
s	**S**ie (*you*)	"z" sound, as in English "*zombie*"
	Hau**s** (*house*)	"ss" sound, as in English "*miss*"

In some German words double "s" is represented by this sign: **ß**

ß	hei**ß**en (*to be called*)	as in English "*super*"
	i**ß**t (*eats*)	as in English "*missed*"
sch	**sch**ön (beautiful)	"sh" sound, as in English "should"
st	**St**adt (*town*)	"sht" sound ("*shtat*")
t	**T**omaten (*tomatoes*)	as in English "*tomatoes*"
th	**Th**eater (*theatre*)	"t" sound, as in English "*tight*"
v	**v**ier (*four*)	"f" sound, as in English "*foot*"
w	**w**o? (*where?*)	"v" sound, as in English "*village*"
z	**Z**igarette (*cigarette*)	"tz" sound, as in "*Ritz*"

NUMBERS AND DATES

 TRY COUNTING FROM 0 TO 12!
Use the pronunciation rules given above and try to read aloud
these German numbers:

0 null	5 fünf	10 zehn
1 eins	6 sechs	11 elf
2 zwei	7 sieben	12 zwölf
3 drei	8 acht	
4 vier	9 neun	

If you can, check the accuracy of your pronunciation by
listening to the tape. Make sure you can recognise numbers
quickly when you hear them spoken. It is also well worth
learning how to write out the numbers.

 FROM 13 TO 20
Look at the numbers below and try to work out how to fill the
gaps; if 13 = **"dreizehn"** ("three ten") then how do you say the
following:

(13 dreizehn)	17 siebz___
14 vier___	18 _____
15 f_____	19 _____
16 sechz___	20 zwanzig

Check your answers with the key on page 16.
Try pronouncing the numbers and check yourself, if
possible, by listening to the tape.

13

FROM 21 TO . . .
Like very old English, German does not say "twenty-one", but "one and twenty".
You should be able to fill in the gaps and then check your answers with the key on page 16.

21	einundzwanzig	31	_____
22	zweiundzwanzig	32	_____
23	dreiundzwanzig	33	_____
24	vierundzwanzig	34	_____
25	fünfundzwanzig	35	_____
26	sechsundzwanzig	36	_____
27	siebenundzwanzig	37	_____
28	achtundzwanzig	38	_____
29	neunundzwanzig	39	_____
30	dreißig	40	vierzig

41	_____	100	hundert/einhundert
42	_____	101	hunderteins
50	fünfzig	102	hundertzwei
60	sechzig	152	hundertzweiundfünfzig
70	siebzig	200	zweihundert
80	_____	300	dreihundert
90	_____	1000	tausend/eintausend

2785 zweitausendsiebenhundertfünfundachtzig

1,000,000 eine Million

Look at the spelling of 2785! It is all one word. You may have to write something like this on a cheque.

THE DAYS OF THE WEEK
Try reading these aloud and then, if you can, check your pronunciation with the tape.

Montag   (*Monday*)
Dienstag   (*Tuesday*)
Mittwoch   (*Wednesday*)
Donnerstag   (*Thursday*)

Freitag	(*Friday*)
Samstag	(*Saturday*)
Sonntag	(*Sunday*)

THE MONTHS OF THE YEAR

Now try the months. They sound more different in German than they look.

Januar	Mai	September
Februar	Juni	Oktober
März	Juli	November
April	August	Dezember

THE FIRST TO THE THIRTY-FIRST

You will need these words especially to talk about dates. Try reading them aloud and then checking your pronunciation as usual, if you can.

on the 1st	am ersten
2nd	zweiten
3rd	dritten
4th	vierten
5th	fünften
6th	sechsten
7th	siebenten
8th	achten
9th	neunten
10th	zehnten
11th	elften
12th	zwölften
13th	dreizehnten
20th	zwanzigsten
21st	einundzwanzigsten

All numbers higher than 20 follow the same rule: to turn them into ordinals, you simply add "**sten**".

DO YOU UNDERSTAND THE DATES?

If you have the tape, listen to the seven dates you will hear, and try to write them down. Check your answers with the key on page 16.

KEY

FROM 13 TO 20
13 dreizehn
14 vierzehn
15 fünfzehn
16 sechzehn
17 siebzehn
18 achtzehn
19 neunzehn
20 zwanzig

FROM 21 TO . . .
31 einunddreißig
32 zweiunddreißig
33 dreiunddreißig
34 vierunddreißig
35 fünfunddreißig
36 sechsunddreißig
37 siebenunddreißig
38 achtunddreißig
39 neununddreißig
41 einundvierzig
42 zweiundvierzig
80 achtzig
90 neunzig

DO YOU UNDERSTAND THE DATES?
Wann sind die Konferenzen? (*When are the meetings?*)
Am ersten Mai, am siebenten Juni, am vierundzwanzigsten Oktober,
am neunzehnten November, am dritten Dezember, am
einundzwanzigsten Dezember, und am vierunddreißigsten Januar.
(*On 1st May, 7th June, 24th October, 19th November, 3rd December, and
34th January.*)
Am vierunddreißigsten Januar?! (*On the 34th January?!*)

2 Introducing Yourself

1. GUTEN TAG!

Waterman: Guten Tag! Mein Name ist John Waterman.
Hello! My name is John Waterman.

Fischer: Fischer.
Fischer.

Waterman: Entschuldigung! Wie ist Ihr Name?
Sorry! What is your name?

Fischer: Fischer. Waltraud Fischer.
Fischer. Waltraud Fischer.

Waterman: Woher kommen Sie?
Where do you come from?

Fischer: Ich komme aus Deutschland. Aus Hannover.
I come from Germany. From Hanover.

Waterman: Ich komme aus England. Aus London.
I come from England. From London.

Fischer: Freut mich!
Pleased to meet you!

1A. HOW IT SOUNDS

Name. Ihr Name. Entschuldigung. Wie ist Ihr Name? Mich. Freut mich!

2. WIE GEHT'S?

Waterman: Guten Morgen, Frau Fischer!
Good morning, Mrs Fischer!

Fischer: Guten Morgen, Herr Waterman! Wie geht's?
Good morning, Mr Waterman! How are you?

Waterman: Gut, danke. Und wie geht es Ihnen?
Well, thank you. And how are you?

Fischer: Danke, es geht.
All right, thank you.

2A. HOW IT SOUNDS

Wie? Wie geht's? Gut, danke. Und wie geht es Ihnen? Es geht.

3. DAS IST FRAU WALLENHORST

Fischer: Hallo, Herr Waterman!
Hello, Mr Waterman!

Waterman: Guten Tag, Frau Fischer!
Hello, Mrs Fischer!

Fischer: Das ist Anke Wallenhorst aus Köln.
This is Anke Wallenhorst from Cologne.

Theis: Nein. Ich bin nicht Anke Wallenhorst. Ich heiße Angela Theis.
No. I am not Anke Wallenhorst. I'm called Angela Theis.

Fischer: Oh, Entschuldigung! Bitte, wie heißen Sie?
Oh, I am sorry! Please, what is your name?

Theis: Angela Theis. Und wer sind Sie?
Angela Theis. And who are you?

Waterman: Ich bin John Waterman aus London.
I am John Waterman from London.

3A. HOW IT SOUNDS

Heißen. Bitte, wie heißen Sie? Und wer sind Sie?

4. WIE IST IHRE ADRESSE?

Theis: Hallo, Herr Waterman! Sie wohnen in London, oder?
Hello, Mr Waterman! You live in London, don't you?

Waterman: Ja, das ist richtig.
Yes, that's right.

Theis: Und wie ist Ihre Adresse?
And what is your address?

Waterman: Meine Adresse ist vierzehn Valetta Road, LONDON W10 7TN.
My address is 14 Valetta Road, LONDON W10 7TN.

Theis: Und wie ist Ihre Telefonnummer?
And what is your telephone number?

Waterman: Die ist null- acht- eins- zwei- vier- drei- fünf- seiben- sechs- neun. Und wie ist Ihre Telefonnummer?
It is 081 243 5769. And what is your telephone number?

Theis: Das sage ich nicht.
I am not saying.

Waterman: Mhm . . .
Mhm . . .

Theis: Na gut, meine Telefonnummer ist null- fünf- eins- drei- sieben- drei- drei- sieben- sieben.
All right, my telephone number is 05137 3377.

Waterman: Noch einmal, bitte langsam.
Could you repeat that, slowly please?

Theis: Null- fünf- eins- drei- sieben- drei- drei- sieben- sieben.
05137 3377.

Waterman: Danke und gute Nacht!
Thank you and good night!

Theis: Gute Nacht!
Good night!

4A. HOW IT SOUNDS

Adresse. Wie ist Ihre Adresse? Telefonnummer. Wie ist Ihre Telefonnummer?
Noch einmal. Noch einmal, bitte langsam. 081. 081 234 5769.

Try to say the numbers as fast as you can. If you don't know the numbers yet, look them up on page 13.

5. WER IST DAS?

Waterman: Wer ist das da?
Who is that over there?
Theis: Das ist David Riley.
That is David Riley.
Waterman: Und woher kommt er?
And where does he come from?
Theis: Er kommt aus England, aber er wohnt in Mallorca.
He comes from England, but he lives in Mallorca.
Waterman: Wie, bitte? Ich verstehe nicht. Wo wohnt er?
Pardon? I don't understand. Where does he live?
Theis: In Mallorca.
In Mallorca.
Waterman: Ah! Und wo arbeitet er?
Ah! And where does he work?
Theis: Bei Siemens.
At Siemens.
Waterman: Ach so. Und wer ist das da?
Ah, right. And who is that over there?
Theis: Das ist Pilar Rodas. Sie wohnt auch in Mallorca.
That is Pilar Rodas. She lives in Mallorca too.

5A. HOW IT SOUNDS

Verstehe. Ich verstehe. Ich verstehe nicht. Wo wohnt er? Und wer ist das da?

6. HALLO!

Frauke: Hallo! Ich bin Frauke. Und wie heißt du?
Hello! I'm Frauke. And what's your name?
Klara: Ich heiße Klara.
My name is Klara.

Frauke: Wie, bitte?
Pardon?
Klara: K-L-A-R-A.
K-L-A-R-A.
Frauke: Und wie alt bist du?
And how old are you?
Klara: Ich bin zehn Jahre alt. Und du?
I'm ten years old. And you?
Frauke: Ich bin neun.
I am nine.

6A. HOW IT SOUNDS
Wie bitte? Bitte, wie heißt du? Und du? Und wie alt bist du?

INFORMATION

SURNAMES AND SHAKING HANDS

If you want to introduce yourself in Germany, you normally just say your surname and shake hands with whomever you are meeting.

When German people answer their telephone at home, they also tend to say their surname first of all.

SIE AND DU

There are two ways of saying "you" in German: the formal "**Sie**" and the informal "**du**". When you first arrive in Germany and you don't know the people you are meeting very well, you should use the formal "**Sie**" until you or the other person decides to change to the informal "**du**". This is normally suggested by either the older person or the woman. However, times are changing and people are becoming more relaxed about these things.

In written German, the formal "you" – "**Sie**" – always has a capital letter.

HOW ARE YOU?

In English people ask "How are you?" or "How do you do?" when they first meet someone. In Germany the enquiry is not made until you meet someone a second time. The question is **"Wie geht's?"** or, more formally, **"Wie geht es Ihnen?"**

LANGUAGE NOTES

I, YOU, HE AND SHE – ICH, SIE, DU, ER AND SIE

These words are called pronouns. Later on you will meet the other pronouns "we" and "they" (page 64) and "it" (page 49).

VERB ENDINGS

In English, we say "I live" but "she lives" – in other words, the ending of the verb (the action or 'doing' word – here, "live") changes depending on the person doing it. In German, the same thing happens.

ich	**-e**	
ich	wohne	in London (*I live in London*)
ich	heiße	Heinz (*I am called Heinz*)
ich	arbeite	bei Siemens (*I work at Siemens*)
Sie	**-en**	
Sie	wohnen	in London (*You live in London*)
Sie	heißen	Waterman (*You are called Waterman*)
Sie	arbeiten	bei Siemens (*You work at Siemens*)
du	**-st**	
du	wohnst	in Deutschland (*You live in Germany*)
du	heißt	Heinz (*You are called Heinz*)
du	arbeitest	in Amerika (*You work in America*)
er/sie	**-t**	
er/sie	wohnt	in Palma de Mallorca (*He/she lives in Palma de Mallorca*)
er/sie	heißt	David/Pilar (*He/she is called David/Pilar*)
er/sie	arbeitet	bei Kodak (*He/she works at Kodak*)

For more on verb endings, see page 25.

TO BE

Most verbs follow a regular pattern of endings like those above, but the German verb "to be" (**sein**) is irregular, so you need to learn:

ich bin Klara (*I am Klara*)
Sie sind intelligent (*You are intelligent*)
du bist sehr intelligent (*You are very intelligent*)
er/sie ist aus England (*He/she is from England*)

ASKING A QUESTION

There are just two types of question in German:

1. Starts with a <u>question word</u>, for instance:
Woher kommen Sie? (*Where do you come from?*)
Wie heißen Sie? (*What are you called?*)
Wo wohnen Sie? (*Where do you live?*)

2. Has <u>the verb at the beginning</u>, for instance:
Sind Sie Frau Wallenhorst? (*Are you Frau Wallenhorst?*)
Kommen Sie aus Berlin? (*Do you come from Berlin?*)
Arbeitet Frau Fischer bei Kodak? (*Does Frau Fischer work at Kodak?*)
Verstehen Sie? (*Do you understand?*)

German questions are therefore simpler than English. German does not make questions like "Do you come from . . . ?" The German question is simply "Come you from . . . ?"

. . . ODER?

The German word "**oder**" means "or". But it is also used at the end of a statement to turn it into a question, like:

Sie sind Herr Waterman, oder? (*You're Mr Waterman, aren't you?*)
Das ist gut, oder? (*That's good, isn't it?*)

YOUR TURN

 1. PRACTISE CONVERSING!
Write down your part in the following conversations and then
compare what you have written with the key on page 27. Also
practise saying your part of the conversations. Doing so is more
fun if you have the **Just Enough German** tapes where the other
parts of the conversations are recorded.

A. INTRODUCE YOURSELF!

You: (Introduce yourself.)
Hauenschild: Hauenschild.
You: (Apologise that you did not get the name and ask for it again.)
Hauenschild: Hauenschild. Dieter Hauenschild.
You: (Ask where he comes from.)
Hauenschild: (Ich komme aus Hamburg. Und Sie?
You: (Tell him where you come from.)

B. HOW ARE YOU?

Schmidt: Guten Morgen! Wie geht's?
You: (Say you are feeling very well and ask about her.)
Schmidt: Danke, es geht.
You: (Introduce Anette Ihssen.)
Schmidt: Freut mich!

C. ADDRESS AND PHONE NUMBER

Schmidt: Sie sind Herr Waterman, oder?
You: (Introduce yourself as Herr Waterman.)
Schmidt: Und wie ist Ihre Adresse?
You: (Give your address.)
Schmidt: Und Ihre Telefonnummer?
You: (Give your telephone number.)

D. WHO IS THAT?

You: (Ask who that is over there.)
Hauenschild: Das ist Pilar Rodas.
You: (Ask where she lives.)
Hauenschild: Sie wohnt in Palma de Mallorca.

2. VERB ENDINGS

Fill in the correct verb endings, then check your answers with the key on page 27.

a) Ich heiß_ Ute Berg.

b) Wo wohn____ Sie?

c) Ich wohn_ in Berlin.

d) Ich versteh_ nicht.

e) Arbeit__ er bei Siemens?

f) Wohn__ Sie in London?

g) Wohn__ sie in Köln?

h) Wer is_ das da?

3. ASKING QUESTIONS

Do you remember how to ask the following questions? Use the formal "Sie".

a) What's your name?
b) Where do you come from?
c) Where do you work?
d) Where do you live?

And:

e) Do you come from England?
f) Are you Mr Fischer?
g) Do you work in London?
h) Do you understand?

Check your translations with the key on page 28.

 ## 4. TELEPHONE NUMBERS

Listen to the dialogues on the tape and try to write down the telephone numbers you will hear. You will probably need to listen several times. Then compare your answers with the key on page 28.

WORD LIST

Abend	evening
Adresse	address
Frau	Mrs
Deutschland	Germany
Herr	Mr
Morgen	morning
Nacht	night
Name	name
Nummer	number
Tag	day
Telefonnummer	telephone number
alt	old
gut	good
langsam	slow, slowly
richtig	correct
sehr	very
aus	from, out of
bei	for, at (a place of work)
da	there
in	in
wer?	who?
wie?	how?
wo?	where?
woher?	where from?

USEFUL EXPRESSIONS

bitte	please
danke	thank you
das ist . . .	that's . . .
Entschuldigung!	Excuse me! Pardon!
Freut mich!	Pleased to meet you!
Es geht	I'm all right
Gute Nacht!	Good night!
Guten Abend!	Good evening!
Guten Morgen!	Good morning!
Guten Tag!	Good day! Germans use this much more than English people. It can be used for "Good morning!" or "Good afternoon" or "Hello!"
Hallo!	Hello!
ich heiße . . .	I am called . . .

26

ich komme aus . . .	I come from . . .
ich verstehe nicht	I don't understand
Mein Name ist . . .	My name is . . .
Na gut . . .	All right . . .
Noch einmal, bitte langsam	Would you repeat that, slowly please?
Wie, bitte?	Pardon? What did you say?
Wie heißen Sie?	What are you called?
Wie ist Ihr Name?	What is your name?
Wie geht's?	How are you?
Wie geht es Ihnen?	How are you? (more formal)

KEY

1A. INTRODUCE YOURSELF!
Ich bin/Ich heiße/Mein Name ist [*your name*].
Entschuldigung! Wie ist Ihr Name?
Woher kommen Sie?
Ich komme aus [*your town or country*].

1B. HOW ARE YOU?
Sehr gut, danke. Und wie geht es Ihnen?
Das ist Anette Ihssen.

1C. ADDRESS AND PHONE NUMBER
Guten Tag! Ich bin/Ich heiße/Mein Name ist John Waterman.
Meine Adresse ist [*your address*].
Meine Telefonnummer ist [*your telephone number*].

1D. WHO IS THAT?
Wer ist das da?
Wo wohnt sie?

2. VERB ENDINGS
a) heiße; b) wohnen; c) wohne; d) verstehe; e) Arbeitet; f) Wohnen;
g) Wohnt; h) ist.

3. QUESTIONS

a) Wie ist Ihr Name?/Wie heißen Sie?
b) Woher kommen Sie?
c) Wo arbeiten Sie?
d) Wo wohnen Sie?
e) Kommen Sie aus England?
f) Sind Sie Herr Fischer?
g) Arbeiten Sie in London?
h) Verstehen Sie?

4. TELEPHONE NUMBERS

Conversation a

Information: Auskunft, Platz vierzehn. (*Information, position 14.*)
Customer: Guten Tag! Die Telefonnummer von Waltraud Brunnenberg in Hannover, bitte. (*Hello! The telephone number of Waltraud Brunnenberg in Hanover, please.*)
Information: Die Telefonnummer ist 05137 206270. (*The number is 05137 206270.*)

Conversation b

Information: Auskunft, Platz fünf. (*Information, position 5.*)
Customer: Guten Tag! Wie ist die Telefonnummer von Frauke Ernst in Bevern, bitte? (*Hello! What is the telephone number of Frauke Ernst in Bevern, please?*)
Information: Die Nummer ist 01513 7414. (*The number is 01513 7414.*)

Conversation c

Information: Auskunft, Platz zwei. (*Information, position 2.*)
Customer: Guten Tag! Die Nummer von Florian Hartung in Berlin, bitte. (*Hello! The number of Florian Hartung in Berlin, please.*)
Information: Moment, bitte. Die Telefonnummer ist 030 7617523. (*One moment, please. The number is 030 7617523.*)

3 At the Hotel

1. HOTEL ATLANTIK

Reception: Hotel Atlantik. Guten Tag!
Hotel Atlantic. Good morning/afternoon!

Guest: Guten Tag! Ich möchte ein Zimmer reservieren.
Good morning/afternoon. I would like to book a room.

Reception: Doppelzimmer oder Einzelzimmer?
Double or single room?

Guest: Ein Doppelzimmer mit Bad, bitte.
A double room with bathroom, please.

Reception: Von wann bis wann kommen Sie?
From when until when are you coming?

Guest: Vom ersten bis siebten April.
From the 1st to the 7th April.

Reception: Moment, bitte . . . Ja, da haben wir noch ein
Doppelzimmer frei. Wie ist Ihr Name?
*One moment, please . . . Yes, we have a double room
free for then. What is your name?*

Guest: Mein Name ist Jane Morgan.
My name is Jane Morgan

Reception: Wie schreibt man das?
How do you spell that?

Guest: J-A-N-E M-O-R-G-A-N.
J-A-N-E M-O-R-G-A-N.

Reception: Und wie ist Ihre Adresse?
And what is your address?

Guest: Meine Adresse ist: Im Dorfe drei,
dreißig- einunddreißig Barsinghausen zwei.
*My address is: Im Dorfe 3,
3031 Barsinghausen 2.*

Reception: Vielen Dank! Auf Wiederhören!
Thank you very much! Goodbye!

Guest: Auf Wiederhören!
Goodbye!

1A. HOW IT SOUNDS

Ich möchte. Ich möchte drei Zimmer. Ich möchte drei Zimmer
reservieren. Doppelzimmer. Einzelzimmer. Doppelzimmer
mit Bad. Schreiben. Man. Wie schreibt man das?

2. RESERVIERUNG

Guest: Guten Tag! Mein Name ist Morgan. Ich habe ein
Doppelzimmer reserviert.
Good morning/afternoon! I've reserved a double room.

Reception: Moment, bitte . . . Ah, ja, hier ist Ihre
Reservierung.
*One moment, please . . . Oh yes. Here is your
reservation.*

Guest: Was kostet das pro Nacht?
What does it cost per night?

Reception: Das kostet hundertfünfzig Mark DM pro Nacht
mit Frühstück.
It costs 150 Deutschmarks per night, with breakfast.

Guest: Vielen Dank!
Thank you very much!

2A. HOW IT SOUNDS

Doppelzimmer. Ich habe ein Doppelzimmer. Ich habe ein
Doppelzimmer reserviert. Frühstück. Das kostet 150 Mark pro
Nacht mit Frühstück.

3. HAT DAS HOTEL EINE SAUNA?

Waterman: Guten Abend! Ich möchte ein Zimmer für eine
Nacht.
Good evening! I would like a room for one night.

Reception: Mit Bad und WC?
With bathroom and toilet?

Waterman: Ja, bitte. Hat das Hotel auch eine Bar?
Yes, please. Does the hotel also have a bar?

Reception: Ja, und ein Schwimmbad, eine Sauna, eine
Disco und eine Sonnenbank.
*Yes, and a swimming pool, a sauna, a disco and a
solarium.*

Waterman: Sehr gut!
Very good!

Reception: Bitte, wie ist Ihr Name?
What is your name, please?

Waterman: Mein Name ist John Waterman.
My name is John Waterman.

Reception: Und Ihre Adresse?
And your address?

Waterman: Vierzehn Valetta Road, London.
14 Valetta Road, London.

Reception: Hier sind Ihre Schlüssel.
Here are your keys.

Waterman: Danke sehr!
Thank you very much!

3A. HOW IT SOUNDS

Auch. Auch eine Bar. Hat das Hotel auch eine Bar?
Schwimmbad. Hat das Hotel auch ein Schwimmbad?

4. WO IST MEIN ZIMMER?

Waterman: Entschuldigung! Wo ist mein Zimmer?
Excuse me! Where is my room?

Reception: Gehen Sie geradeaus den Korridor entlang bis zum Restaurant, dann links und dann sofort wieder rechts. Da ist Zimmer Nummer acht.
Go straight along the corridor as far as the restaurant, then left and then immediately right. And there you will find Room 8.

Waterman: Vielen Dank! Und wo ist die Sauna?
Many thanks! And where is the sauna?

Reception: Hier ist der Lift. Die Sauna and das Schwimmbad sind in der vierten Etage.
Here is the lift. The sauna and the swimming pool are on the fourth floor.

Waterman: Vielen Dank!
Many thanks!

4A. HOW IT SOUNDS

Gehen Sie rechts. Gehen Sie links. Gehen Sie geradeaus. Gehen Sie geradeaus den Korridor entlang. In der vierten Etage. Die Sauna und das Schwimmbad sind in der vierten Etage.

5. ICH MÖCHTE BEZAHLEN

Waterman: Guten Morgen! Ich möchte bezahlen.
Good morning! I would like to pay my bill.

Reception: Guten Morgen, Herr Waterman! Wie ist Ihre Zimmernummer?
Good morning, Mr Waterman! What is your room number?

Waterman: Zimmer Nummer acht.
Room number 8.

Reception: Das macht hundert Mark inclusive Mehrwertsteuer für das Einzelzimmer.
That's 100 Marks including VAT, for the single room.

Waterman: Kann ich mit Kreditkarte bezahlen?
Can I pay by credit card?

Reception:	Selbstverständlich. Hier ist Ihre Rechnung. Unterschreiben Sie hier unten, bitte!
	Of course. Here is your bill. Sign at the bottom here, please!
Waterman:	Wiedersehen und vielen Dank!
	Goodbye and many thanks!
Reception:	Danke auch. Gute Reise!
	Thank you, too. Have a good journey.

5A. HOW IT SOUNDS

Ich möchte bezahlen. Steuer. Mehrwertsteuer. Inclusive Mehrwertsteuer. Kreditkarte. Kann ich mit Kreditkarte bezahlen? Selbstverständlich. Rechnung. Hier ist Ihre Rechnung.

INFORMATION

WHERE TO STAY

In Germany you can stay in a 'Hotel', 'Gasthof' or 'Pension'. In a Hotel you may choose between full board (**Vollpension**) or half board (**Halbpension**) or just stay overnight and have breakfast (**Frühstück**) in the morning. At a Gasthof, the main business is a Restaurant (**Restaurant**) or a pub (**Kneipe**), but you can stay overnight there too. It is usually cheaper and of a lower standard than a hotel. A Pension is the equivalent of bed and breakfast accommodation in Britain.

If you need a list of local hotels, B&Bs, or just information, go to the local tourist office (**Fremdenverkehrsbüro**) – which you'll find in any town or area of interest.

MONEY MATTERS

In Germany, as in England, there are three ways of paying your bill: in cash, by cheque or by credit card. But don't rely too much on the latter. Surprising though it may seem, the harsh reality is that there are lots of places (even some very good hotels and restaurants) which don't accept credit cards. Make sure you have some cash and Eurocheques, which are accepted almost everywhere.

LANGUAGE NOTES

DER, DIE OR DAS? – THE

You have probably noticed these three different words for "the" in German. **"Der"**, **"die"** and **"das"** are used, depending on the gender of the noun that follows. In German, every noun is masculine or feminine or neuter. For instance:

masculine: **der Massageraum** (*massage room*)
feminine: **die Bar** (*bar*)
neuter: **das Zimmer** (*room*)

How can you tell if a noun is masculine, feminine or neuter? There is some bad news here: there are very few reliable rules. You really have to learn the "article" (i.e. **"der"**, **"die"** or **"das"**) with every noun. Do not worry too much: everyone will still understand you if you do not get the articles right. You can decide for yourself how much you want to focus on this.

SINGULAR AND PLURAL – JUST ONE OR MORE THAN ONE?

When you are talking about more than one thing, the word for "the" is **"die"**, whatever the gender of the noun. So that is easy!

singular   plural
der Massageraum   **die Massageräume**
(*the massage room*)   (*the massage rooms*)
die Bar (*the bar*)   **die Bars** (*the bars*)
das Zimmer (*the room*)   **die Zimmer** (*the rooms*)

What is not so easy is the way nouns sometimes change slightly in the plural. **"Die Massageräume"** gets an umlaut. **"Die Bars"** gets an "s" on the end. **"Die Zimmer"** is not changed from the singular **"das Zimmer"**. When you learn new nouns and their articles, you can learn the plural, too. But again, you can decide how much you want to focus on this. It is more important for writing German correctly.

CAPITAL LETTERS

Have you noticed that, in German, every noun is written with a capital letter at the beginning?

EIN – A

"The" is called the definite article and has been explained in the previous notes; "a" (or "an") is the <u>indefinite article</u>. In German, this also changes according to the gender of the noun that follows – **"ein"**, **"eine"** or **"ein"**:

masculine: **ein Massageraum** (*a massage room*)
feminine: **eine Bar** (*a bar*)
neuter: **ein Zimmer** (*a room*)

There is no plural of "a", so the plurals of the above three words are simply:

Massageräume (*massage rooms*)
Bars (*bars*)
Zimmer (*rooms*)

MEIN, DEIN AND IHR – MY AND YOUR

"**Mein**" means "my", "**dein**" means "your" when said informally, and "**Ihr**" (with a capital "I") is the formal "your". (Apply the same rules regarding formal/informal modes of address as given earlier for **"Sie"** and **"du"**.)
All three words, **"Mein"**, **"dein"** and **"Ihr"**, follow the same pattern as "**ein**" in the singular, but they also have a plural:

"**der Name**" is a masculine noun. Therefore:
mein Name (*My name*)
dein Name (*Your name*) – informal
Ihr Name (*Your name*) – formal

"**die Adresse**" is a feminine noun. Therefore:
meine Adresse (*My address*)
deine Adresse (*Your address*) – informal
Ihre Adresse (*Your address*) – formal

"**das Zimmer**" is a neuter noun. Therefore:
mein Zimmer (*My room*)
dein Zimmer (*Your room*) – informal
Ihr Zimmer (*Your room*) – formal

"die Namen" is plural. Therefore:
meine Namen (*My names*)
deine Namen (*Your names*) – informal
Ihre Namen (*Your names*) – formal

YOUR TURN

1. PRACTISE CONVERSING!

Write down your part of the conversation and then compare it with the key on page 41. Also practise speaking your part, which will be easier with the **Just Enough German** tape.

A. RESERVE A DOUBLE ROOM

Reception: Hotel Harenberger Hof. Guten Tag!
You: (Greet the receptionist and say you would like to reserve a double room.)
Reception: Von wann bis wann?
You: (From 1st to 10th April.)
Reception: Ja. Da haben wir noch ein Zimmer frei.
You: (Ask the price of the room.)
Reception: Hundert Mark das Doppelzimmer mit Frühstück.
You: (Say all right. You would like to reserve the room.)
Reception: Wie ist Ihr Name, bitte?
You: (Say your name.)
Reception: Und Ihre Adresse?
You: (Give your address.)
Reception: Gut. Das Zimmer ist für Sie reserviert.
You: (Say thank you and goodbye.)

B. AT THE HOTEL

Reception: Guten Morgen!
You: (Greet the receptionist and tell her that you have reserved a room for one night.)
Reception: Wie ist Ihr Name, bitte?
You: (Give your name.)
Reception: Wie schreibt man das?
You: (Spell your name.)
Reception: Ja. Hier ist Ihre Reservierung. Sie haben Zimmer Nummer acht.

You: (Ask where the room is.)
Reception: Gehen Sie hier rechts, dann geradeaus. Da ist Zimmer Nummer acht.
You: (Say thanks.)

2. SPELL THE NAMES
Listen to the conversations on the tape, in which you will hear people spelling their names, and see if you can write down these names. (If you need to, revise the alphabet, in chapter 1.)

3. DER, DIE OR DAS?
Write the correct article in front of each word:

a) ___ Schlüssel

b) ___ Adresse

c) ___ Telefonnummer

d) ___ Zimmer

e) ___ Hotel

f) ___ Pensionen

4. EIN OR EINE?
Write the correct form of "**ein**" in front of each word:

a) ___ Namen

b) ___ Bar

c) ___ Massageraum

d) ___ Doppelzimmer

e) ___ Problem

f) ___ Rechnung

5. MEIN, IHR, DEIN
Write the correct form of the correct word in the gaps:

a) Entschuldigung! Ist das___ (*formal your*) Zimmer?

b) Ja. Das ist ___ (*my*) Zimmer.

c) Hier ist ___ (*formal your*) Rechnung.

d) Das ist nicht ___ (*my*) Problem.

e) Wo ist ___ (*informal your*) Kreditkarte?

WORD LIST

From this chapter onwards,
the Word List shows the gender of
each noun and its plural form in brackets

das Bad (-er)	bath (baths)
die Bar (-s)	bar
die Disco (-s)	disco
das Doppelzimmer	double room
die Dusche (-n)	shower
das Einzelzimmer	single room
die Etage (-n)	floor, storey
das Fremdenverkehrsbüro (-s)	tourist office
das Frühstück (-e)	breakfast
die Garage (-n)	garage, parking
der Gasthof (-höfe)	restaurant
die Halbpension	half board
das Hotel (-s)	hotel
der Konferenzraum (-räume)	conference room
der Korridor (-e)	corridor
die Kneipe (-n)	pub
die Kreditkarte (-n)	credit card
der Lift (-s or -e)	lift
der Massageraum (-räume)	massage room
die Mehrwertsteuer (-n)	VAT
die Nummer (-n)	number
der Parkplatz (-plätze)	parking
die Pension (-en)	guest house
das Problem (-e)	problem
die Rechnung (-en)	bill
die Reise (-n)	journey
die Reservierung (-en)	reservation
das Restaurant (-s)	restaurant
die Sauna (-s)	sauna
der Schlüssel	key
das Schwimmbad (-er)	swimming pool
die Sonnenbank (-e)	solarium
die Vollpension	full board
das WC	toilet
das Zimmer	room
bezahlen	to pay
kosten	to cost
reservieren	to reserve

auch	also
bis	until
dann	then
⟍entlang	along
frei	free
für	for
⟍geradeaus	straight out
⟍hier unten	under here
inclusive	including
links	left
mit	with, by
noch	still
pro	for, per
rechts	right
sofort	straightaway
wieder	again

USEFUL EXPRESSIONS

Auf Wiederhören!	Goodbye (on the phone)
Auf Wiedersehen!	Goodbye
Das macht . . .	That makes . . .
Gehen Sie . . .	Go . . .
Gute Reise!	Have a good journey!
Hier ist . . .	Here is . . .
Ich möchte . . .	I would like to . . .
Ja	Yes
Kann ich . . .	Can I . . .
Kann ich mit Kreditkarte bezahlen?	Can I pay by credit card?
Moment, bitte	Just a moment
Selbstverständlich	Of course
Unterschreiben Si hier unten bitte	Sign below here please
Von wann bis wann?	From when till when?
Was kostet . . . ?	What does . . . cost?
Wie schreibt man das?	How do you spell that?

1A. RESERVE A DOUBLE ROOM
Guten Tag! Ich möchte ein Doppelzimmer reservieren.
Vom ersten bis zehnten April.
Was kostet das Zimmer? OR Was kostet das?
Gut. Ich möchte das Zimmer reservieren.
Mein Name ist [*your name*]. OR Ich heiße [*your name*].
Meine Adresse ist [*your address*].
Vielen Dank!/Danke sehr! Auf Wiedersehen!

1B. AT THE HOTEL
Guten Tag! Ich habe ein Zimmer für eine Nacht reserviert.
Mein Name ist [*your name*]. OR Ich heiße [*your name*].
[*Spell your name.*]
Wo ist mein Zimmer?
Vielen Dank!

2. SPELL THE NAMES
Wie ist Ihr Name?
Mein Name ist (a) Ute Berg; (b) Dieter Hauenschild; (c) Klara
Wasserberg; (d) Frauke de Vries; (e) Fritz Schünemann.
Und wie schreibt man das?

3. DER, DIE OR DAS?
a) der Schlüssel (*singular*) or die Schlüssel (*plural*)
b) die Adresse
c) die Telefonnummer
d) das Zimmer
e) das Hotel
f) die Pensionen (= *plural*)

4. EIN OR EINE?
a) Namen (= *plural*)
b) eine Bar
c) ein Doppelzimmer
d) ein Problem
e) eine Rechnung

5. MEIN, IHR, DEIN
a) Ihr Zimmer
b) mein Zimmer
c) Ihre Rechnung
d) mein Problem
e) deine Kreditkarte

4 Going Shopping

1. WAS KOSTET . . . ?

Customer: Guten Morgen! Was kostet eine Flasche Bier?
Good morning! How much is a bottle of beer?

Shopkeeper: Eine Mark fünfundvierzig.
1.45 DM.

Customer: Und ein Kilo Wurst?
And a kilo of cold meat/sausage?

Shopkeeper: Vierundzwanzig Mark dreißig die Salami,
neunzehn Mark fünfzig die Bratwurst, siebzehn
Mark fünfzig die Teewurst, achtzehn Mark
fünfunddreißig die Leberwurst.
*24.30 DM for the salami, 19.50 for the Bratwurst,
17.50 for the Teewurst, 18.35 DM for the liver
sausage.*

Customer: Hmmm. Und was kostet ein Apfel?
Hmmm. And how much is an apple?

Shopkeeper: Neunzig Pfennig.
90 pfennig.

Customer: Das ist aber teuer! Und wieviel kostet ein Liter
Orangensaft?
*That's really expensive! And how much is a litre of
orange juice?*
Shopkeeper: Eine Mark dreißig.
1.30 DM.
Customer: Oh, das ist aber billig! Und was kostet eine
Packung Zigaretten?
*Oh, that's really cheap! And how much is a packet of
cigarettes?*
Shopkeeper: Fünf Mark zwanzig.
5.20 DM

1A. HOW IT SOUNDS
90 Pfennig. Eine Mark dreißig (1.30 DM). Einundzwanzig
Mark fünfzig (21.50 DM). Siebenhundertfvierundfünfzig
Mark siebenundsechzig (754.67 DM).
Dreitausendneunhundertsechsundsiebzig Mark
dreiunddreißig DeutschMark (3976.33 DM). Das ist aber teuer!
Oh, das ist aber billig!

2. ICH NEHME EINE FLASCHE BIER
Customer: Gut. Dann nehme ich einen Liter Orangensaft,
einen Liter Milch, eine Flasche Bier und eine
Packung Zigaretten.
*Good. Then I'll take a litre of orange juice, a litre of
milk, a bottle of beer and a packet of cigarettes.*
Shopkeeper: Sonst noch etwas?
Anything else?
Customer: Und das da, bitte. Wie heißt das auf deutsch?
*And that there please. What is that called in
German?*
Shopkeeper: Das ist ein Pizzaboden.
That is a pizza base.
Customer: Gut! Und einen Pizzaboden, zwei Paprika und
hundert Gramm Salami, bitte.
*Good! A pizza base, two peppers and 100 grammes
of salami, please.*
Shopkeeper: Bitteschön.
There you are.

Customer: Und ich hätte gern noch zweihundert Gramm Käse, zweihundertfünfzig Gramm Champignons, eine Dose Tomaten und eine Tüte Chips.
And I would also like 200 grammes of cheese, 250 grammes of mushrooms, a tin of tomatoes and a bag of crisps.

Shopkeeper: Tut mir leid, aber wir haben keine Chips.
I'm sorry, but we don't have any crisps.

Customer: Dann möchte ich eine Tüte Erdnüsse. Das ist alles.
Then I would like a bag of peanuts. That's all.

Shopkeeper: Das macht zusammen zwanzig Mark fünfzig.
That makes 20.50 DM altogether.

Customer: Bitte.
Here you are.

Shopkeeper: Vielen Dank! Auf Wiedersehen!
Thank you! Goodbye!

Customer: Auf Wiedersehen!

2A. HOW IT SOUNDS

Ich nehme. Dann nehme ich. Dann nehme ich eine Flasche Bier. Ich hätte gern. Ich hätte gern eine Tüte Chips. Das ist alles.

3. DER PULLOVER IST ABER SCHÖN!

Customer: Der Pullover ist aber schön!
The pullover is really beautiful!

Friend: Findest du?
Do you think so?

Customer: Guten Tag!
Good morning/afternoon!

Shopkeeper: Guten Tag! Bitteschön!
Good morning/afternoon! Can I help you?

Customer: Haben Sie den Pullover hier in Größe vierzig?
Have you got this pullover in size 40?

Shopkeeper: Ja hier, bitte.
Yes, here you are.

Customer: Wo kann ich ihn anprobieren?
Where can I try it on?

Shopkeeper: Hier ist die Umkleidekabine . . . Paßt der
Pullover?
Here is the changing room . . . Does the pullover fit?
Customer: Ja. Vielen Dank! Ich nehme ihn.
Yes. Thank you! I'll take it.

3A. HOW IT SOUNDS
Pullover. Oh, der Pullover. Oh, der Pullover ist aber schön!
Größe 40. Haben Sie Größe 40? Haben Sie den Pullover in
Größe 40? Anprobieren. Wo kann ich ihn anprobieren? Ich
nehme ihn.

4. GEÖFFNET ODER GESCHLOSSEN?
Man: Ist die Apotheke geöffnet?
Is the chemist open?
Woman: Nein, die ist geschlossen.
No, it is shut.
Man: Und der Supermarkt? Hat der offen?
And the supermarket. Is it open?
Woman: Nein, auch nicht.
No, also not.
Man: Die Bäckerei, ist die offen?
The baker's, is it open?
Woman: Nein, nein.
No, no.
Man: Was hat denn heute offen?
What is open today then?
Woman: Nichts. Alle Geschäfte sind zu. Heute ist doch
Sonntag!
*Nothing. All the shops are closed. Today is Sunday,
after all!*

4A. HOW IT SOUNDS
Apotheke. Supermarkt. Geöffnet. Geschlossen. Ist die
Apotheke geöffnet? Auch. Auch nicht. Nein, der Supermarkt
auch nicht. Es ist Sonntag. Es ist doch Sonntag!

INFORMATION

WHAT TO BUY

Food shopping can be exciting. You should try all the different
types of sausages (**Würst**) and cold cuts (**Schinken, Kassler**,
etc), and the vast range of breads (**Brot**), rolls (**Brötchen**),
cakes (**Kuchen**) and biscuits (**Kekse**), not to mention the beer
(**Bier**)!

HOW MUCH TO BUY

If you aren't already, you will need to become familiar with
metric weights and measurements, to say how much of
something you want to buy. Here are some approximate
equivalents you will probably find useful:

lengths:
1 inch = about 3 cm: **drei Zentimeter**
6 inches = about 15 cm: **fünfzehn Zentimeter**
1 foot = about 30 cm: **dreißig Zentimeter**
1 yard = about 1 metre: **ein Meter**

weights:
1 ounce = about 30 grams: **dreißig Gramm**
4 ounces = about 115 grams: **hundertfünfzehn Gramm**
8 ounces = about 250 grams: **zweihundertfünfzig Gramm**
1 pound = about 0.5 kilogramme: **ein halbes Kilogramm, or
ein halbes Kilo**
2 pounds = about 1 kilogramme: **ein Kilogramm, or ein Kilo**

capacity:
half a pint = about quarter of a litre/25 centilitres:
fünfundzwanzig Zentiliter
1 pint = about half a litre: **ein halbes Liter**
2 pints = about 1 litre: **ein Liter**

To say "about", say "**ungefähr**".

SHOPPING FOR CLOTHES

Here are the sizes you will find in Germany for clothes and shoes:

Women's clothes:

UK	8	10	12	14	16	18	20			
Germany	34	36	38	40	42	44	46			

Men's clothes:

UK	36	38	40	42	44	46				
Germany	46	48	50	52	54	56				

Shoes:

UK	2½	3½	4	5	5½	6	7	8	9	10	11
Germany	35	36	37	38	39	40	41	42	43	44	45

WHERE AND WHEN TO SHOP

Each town has a pedestrian area in the centre, where you can find almost everything you want, and where you won't be bothered by traffic. If you are driving, just leave your car in a nearby car park.

Do not rely on your credit cards, as small shops and supermarkets might not accept them.

Opening hours differ between larger towns and the country. In large towns, the shops are open:

Montag	9.00 – 18.30
Dienstag	9.00 – 18.30
Mittwoch	9.00 – 18.30
Donnerstag	9.00 – 20.30
Freitag	9.00 – 18.30
Samstag	9.00 – 14.00*

*But on the first Saturday of every month, the shops are open until 18.00.

In the country, the shops are open:

Montag	9.00 – 13.00; 15.00 – 18.00
Dienstag	9.00 – 13.00; 15.00 – 18.00
Mittwoch	9.00 – 13.00
Donnerstag	9.00 – 13.00; 15.00 – 18.00
Freitag	9.00 – 13.00; 15.00 – 18.00
Samstag	9.00 – 12.30

DANKE AND BITTESCHÖN

There are lots of ways to say "thank you". Here is a small selection:

Danke
Danke schön
Danke sehr
Vielen Dank
Tausend Dank

"**Bitte**" means "please", but also "**bitte**" or "**bitteschön**" means "There you are" or "Can I take your order?"

LANGUAGE NOTES

SUBJECTS AND OBJECTS

The subject of a sentence is the "doer", and the "doer" can be a person or a thing (e.g. **Klara, ich, das Bier**). In the following examples, the subject is underlined:

<u>Ich</u> wohne in London. (*<u>I</u> live in London.*)
<u>Das Bier</u> ist kalt. (*<u>The beer</u> is cold.*)
<u>Der Mann</u> hat den Schlüssel. (*<u>The man</u> has the key.*)

The object of a sentence is the "inactive element" – the person who, or the thing which, has something done to it. For example (the object being underlined):

Der Mann hat <u>den Schlüssel.</u> (*The man has <u>the key</u>.*)
Sie nehmen <u>eine Packung</u> Zigaretten. (*You take <u>a packet</u> of cigarettes.*)
Ich liebe <u>Heinz</u> .(*I love <u>Heinz.</u>*)

NOMINATIVE AND ACCUSATIVE

These are the grammatical terms for subject and object. In the sentence "**Der Mann hat den Schlüssel**", "**Der Mann**" is in the <u>nominative case</u> and "**den Schlüssel**" is in the <u>accusative case</u>.

Later on we will meet another case, the dative (see page 93).

DER, DIE, DAS AND EIN, EINE

To speak German really correctly, you need to understand and remember the difference between subjects and objects, because there are rules about the endings of the definite articles ("**der**","**die**", "**das**", "**die**") and the indefinite articles ("**ein**", "**eine**", "**ein**"), depending on whether they are in front of the subject or object of a sentence.

	Subject Nominative	Object Accusative
Masculine	**der**	**den**
Feminine	**die**	**die**
Neuter	**das**	**das**
Plural	**die**	**die**
Masculine	**ein**	**einen**
Feminine	**eine**	**eine**
Neuter	**ein**	**ein**

You will see that it is not so difficult as it may sound, since it is only the masculine forms of the articles that change.

THE PRONOUN "IT"

Because nouns in German are either masculine, feminine or neuter, the word for "it" takes different forms.

	Subject Nominative	Object Accusative
der Schlüssel	**er**	**ihn**
die Packung	**sie**	**sie**
Das Bier	**es**	**es**

Of course, "**er**" and "**sie**" also mean *he* and *she*. And "**ihn**" and "**sie**" mean *him* and *her*.

ABER!

The word "**aber**" means *but*. However it is also used to express surprise, as in:

Das ist aber billig!
Das ist aber schön!

1. GO SHOPPING!
Write down your part of the conversation and compare it with the key on page 55. Also practise speaking your part, with the tape if possible.

Shopkeeper: Guten Morgen!
You: (Greet the shopkeeper and ask the price of a litre of whisky.)
Shopkeeper: Ein Liter Whisky kostet 17.5 DM.
You: (Say all right and that you'd like a litre. Then ask the price of 100 grammes of salami.)
Shopkeeper: 1.98 DM.
You: (Say "yes please" and then ask "What's that over there?")
Shopkeeper: Das ist Schwarzwälderkirschtorte (Black Forest gâteau).
You: (Ask for one.)
Shopkeeper: Sonst noch etwas?
You: (Say "no thank you".)
Shopkeeper: Das macht 45.30 DM.
You: (Say "here you are".)
Shopkeeper: Vielen Dank and auf Wiedersehen!
You: (Say goodbye.)

Aus unserem Getränkemarkt:

Franziskaner Hefeweißbier
Hell oder **Dunkel**
20 Flaschen à
0,5 Liter
Kasten (zzgl.
DM 6,– Pfand) **20.⁹⁹**

Erdinger Hefeweißbier
Hell oder **Dunkel**
20 Fl. à 0,5 Liter
Kasten (zzgl.
DM 6,– Pfand) **21.⁹⁹**

2. WHAT PRICE?

Prices, like any numbers, are difficult to understand in a foreign language. Listen to the tape and write down the prices you hear. Then check your answers with the key on page 55.

3. THINGS TO BUY

Look up the meanings, genders and plurals of the following words and fill in the correct article: **der**, **die** or **das**:

a) ___ Briefmarke

b) ___ Postkarte

c) ___ Brot

d) ___ Fahrkarte

e) ___ Computer

f) ___ T-shirt

g) ___ Hose

h) ___ Kleid

i) ___ Film

j) ___ Flasche

k) ___ Eis

51

4. BUY ONE!

Now buy the items in exercise 3: fill in the correct, accusative (object) form of the article: **den**, **die**, **das**, **einen**, **eine**, **ein**.

a) Ich möchte ___ Briefmarke

b) Ich möchte ___ Postkarte

c) Ich möchte ___ Brot

d) Ich möchte ___ Fahrkarte

e) Ich möchte ___ Computer

f) Ich möchte ___ T-shirt

g) Ich möchte ___ Hose

h) Ich möchte ___ Kleid

i) Ich möchte ___ Film

j) Ich möchte ___ Flasche Whisky

k) Ich möchte ___ Eis

5. SPECIAL OFFER PRICES!

Listen to the tape (or look at the adverts on the previous page) and write down the prices of those items which are on special offer. It's a better exercise if you can do this by listening – and of course you should write the prices in full, not in figures!

a) Nürnberger Rostbratwürstchen

b) Fleischwurst

c) Vienetta

d) Bavariablu

e) Iglo Gemüse

f) Franziskaner Hefeweißbier

g) Erdinger Hefeweißbier

WORD LIST

der Apfel (Äpfel)	apple
die Apotheke (-n)	chemist, pharmacy
die Bäckerei (-en)	baker's
das Bier (-e)	beer
die Bratwurst (-würste)	type of sausage
die Briefmarke (-n)	stamp
das Brot (-e)	bread
das Brötchen	roll
der Champignon (-s)	white mushroom
die Chips (= plural)	crisps
der Computer	computer
die Dose (-n)	tin
das Eis	ice cream
die Erdnuß (-nüsse)	peanut
die Fahrkarte (-n)	ticket
der Film (-e)	film
die Flasche (-n)	bottle
das Geschäft (-e)	shop
das Gramm (-e)	gramme
die Größe (-n)	size
die Hose (-n)	pair of trousers
der Käse	cheese
der Keks (-e)	biscuit
das Kilo	kilogram
das Kleid (-er)	dress
der Kuchen	cake
die Leberwurst (-würste)	liver sausage
das Liter	litre
die Mark	mark (currency)
die Milch	milk
der Orangensaft (-säfte)	orange juice
die Packung (-en)	packet
die Paprika	red, green or yellow pepper
der Pfennig (-e)	German pfennig (one-hundreth of a mark)
der Pizzaboden	pizza base
die Postkarte (-n)	postcard
der Pullover	pullover
die Salami (-s)	salami

der Schinken	ham
die Schwarzwalderkirschtorte (-n)	Black Forest gâteau
der Supermarkt (-märkte)	supermarket
die Teewurst (-würste)	type of sausage
die Tomate (-n)	tomato
das T-shirt (-s)	T-shirt
die Tüte (-n)	plastic bag
die Umkleidekabine (-n)	changing room
der Whisky	whisky
die Wurst (Würste)	sausage
Die Zigarette (-n)	cigarette
anprobieren	to try on
finden	to find
nehmen	to take
passen	to fit
alles	everything
billig	cheap
etwas	something
geöffnet	open
geschlossen	shut, closed
heute	today
kalt	cold
offen	open
schön	beautiful, lovely
sonst	otherwise, else
teuer	expensive
ungefähr	about
zusammen	together

USEFUL EXPRESSIONS

Das ist alles	That's all
Das macht zusammen . . .	That makes . . . altogether
Ich hätte gern . . .	I would like . . .
Ist . . . geöffnet?	Is . . . open?
Sonst noch etwas?	Anything else?
Tut mir leid	I am sorry
Was kostet . . . ?	What does . . . cost?/ How much is . . . ?
Wieviel kostet . . . ?	How much is . . . ?

1. GO SHOPPING!
Guten Morgen! Was kostet ein Liter Whisky?
Gut. Ich möchte einen Liter. Und was kosten 100 Gramm Salami?
100 Gramm bitte. Und was ist das da?
Eine bitte.
Nein, danke.
Bitte.
Auf Wiedersehen!

 2. WHAT PRICE?
2.00 DM; 22 DM; 4.10 DM; 12.60 DM; 37.50 DM; 18.98 DM; 200.00 DM; 44.22 DM; 1087.90 DM.

3. THINGS TO BUY
a) **die** Briefmarke (-n) *stamp*
b) **die** Postkarte (-n) *postcard*
c) **das** Brot (-e) *bread*
d) **die** Fahrkarte (-n) *ticket*
e) **der** Computer *computer*
f) **das** T-shirt (-s) *T-shirt*
g) **die** Hose (-n) *pair of trousers*
h) **das** Kleid (-er) *dress*
i) **der** Film (-e) *film*
j) **die** Flasche (-n) *bottle*
k) **das** Eis *ice cream*

4. BUY ONE!
a) Ich möchte **eine** Briefmarke
b) Ich möchte **eine** Postkarte
c) Ich möchte **ein** Brot
d) Ich möchte **eine** Fahrkarte
e) Ich möchte **einen** Computer
f) Ich möchte **ein** T-shirt
g) Ich möchte **eine** Hose
h) Ich möchte **ein** Kleid
i) Ich möchte **einen** Film
j) Ich möchte **eine** Flasche Whisky
k) Ich möchte **ein** Eis.

5. SPECIAL OFFER PRICES!

Heute finden Sie bei uns im Angebot: (*Today we have on special offer:*)
Nürnberger Rostbratwürstchen – die 200 Gramm Packung für nur
2.99.
Fleischwurst – die 650 Gramm Packung für nur 2.99.
Vienetta, zartes Blättereis – 500 Gramm für 2.29.
Bavariablu – 100 Gramm heute für nur 1.99.
Iglo Gemüse – Brokoli, Rahm-Porree oder Apfel-Rotkohl – die
Packung für 2.29.
Und aus dem Getränkemarkt: (*And from the drinks counter:*)
Franziskaner Hefeweißbier – hell oder dunkel – der Kasten für 20.99.
Oder Erdinger Weizen – hell oder dunkel – für sensationelle 21.99.

5 At the Restaurant

1. ICH MÖCHTE EINEN TISCH RESERVIEREN

Reception: Restaurant Harenberger Hof. Guten Tag!

Restaurant: *Harenberger Hof. Hello!*

Customer: Guten Tag! Ich möchte einen Tisch für heute abend reservieren.
Hello! I would like to book a table for this evening.

Reception: Für wieviele Personen?
For how many people?

Customer: Für vier.
For four.

Reception: Um wieviel Uhr kommen Sie?
What time are you coming?

Customer: Um acht Uhr.
At 8 o'clock.

Reception: Und wie ist Ihr Name?
And what is your name?

Customer: Uebel.
Uebel.

Reception: Gut. Der Tisch ist für Sie reserviert.
All right. The table is reserved for you.
Customer: Vielen Dank!
Many thanks!

1A. HOW IT SOUNDS

Restaurant. Tisch. Ich möchte einen Tisch reservieren. Ich möchte einen Tisch für heute abend reservieren. Uhr. Um wieviel Uhr? Um ein Uhr. Um zwei Uhr. Um drei Uhr. Um vier Uhr. Um fünf Uhr.

2. DIE KARTE BITTE!

Dieter: Herr Ober, die Karte bitte!
Waiter, the menu please!
Waiter: Bitteschön.
Here you are.
Dieter: So, was nehmt ihr?
So what are you having?
Ute: Mhm. Ich nehme als Vorspeise die Tomatensuppe und dann ein Wiener Schnitzel.
Mhm. I'll have tomato soup for starter and then a Wiener Schnitzel.
Heinz: Das nehme ich auch. Und was ißt du?
I'll have the same. And what are you eating?
Dieter: Ich glaube, ich esse zuerst eine Zwiebelsuppe und als Hauptgericht nehme ich die Forelle blau mit Kartoffeln und Salat.
I think I'll have onion soup first and as main course trout with potatoes and salad.
Frauke: Mhm, lecker! Die Zwiebelsuppe möchte ich auch und danach ein Rumpsteak mit gebackene Kartoffel und Kräuterbutter. Und dazu grüne Bohnen.
Mhm, delicious! I'd like the onion soup too, followed by rump steak with a baked potato and herb butter. And green beans as well.
Dieter: Und was trinken wir? Weißwein oder Rotwein?
And what shall we drink? White or red wine?

Ute: Warum nehmen wir nicht eine Flasche
Weißwein und eine Flasche Rotwein?
*Why not have one bottle of white and one bottle of
red wine?*

Dieter and Frauke: Gute Idee!
Good idea!

Heinz: Ich möchte lieber ein Glas Bier.
I'd rather have a glass of beer.

2A. HOW IT SOUNDS

Die Karte. Herr Ober, die Karte bitte! Als Vorspeise. Ich
nehme als Vorspeise. Ich nehme als Vorspeise die
Tomatensuppe. Als Hauptgericht. Ich nehme als Hauptgericht
ein Rumpsteak mit Kräuterbutter. Trinken. Was trinken wir?
Weißwein. Rotwein. Ich trinke ein Glas Bier. Ich möchte lieber
ein Glas Bier.

3. HERR OBER, WIR MÖCHTEN BESTELLEN!

Dieter: Herr Ober, wir möchten bestellen!
Waiter, we would like to order!

Waiter: Bitteschön!
Yes, what would you like?

Dieter: Wir hätten gern eine Flasche Rotwein, eine
Flasche Weißwein und ein Glas Bier.
*We would like a bottle of red wine, a bottle of white
wine and a glass of beer.*

Waiter: Groß oder klein?
Large or small?

Dieter: Groß bitte. Und zweimal die Tomatensuppe und
zwei Zwiebelsuppen. Dann hätten wir gern
zweimal das Wiener Schnitzel mit Bratkartoffeln
und Gemüse, eine Forelle blau mit Kartoffeln
und Salat und ein Rumpsteak mit gebackener
Kartoffel und Kräuterbutter.
*Large please. And tomato soup twice and two onion
soups. Then we would like Wiener Schnitzel twice
with fried potatoes and vegetables, the trout with
potatoes and salad, and a rump steak with a baked
potato and herb butter.*

Waiter: Möchten Sie das Steak englisch, medium oder durchgebraten?
Would you like the steak rare, medium or well-done?

Frauke: Medium bitte.
Medium please.

Waiter: Und möchten Sie den Hauswein?
And would you like the house wine?

Dieter: Ja, bitte.
Yes, please.

3A. HOW IT SOUNDS

Wir hätten gern Wein. Wir hätten gern eine Flasche Hauswein. Groß. Klein. Groß oder klein? Steak. Steak mit Salat. Kartoffeln. Steak mit Salat und Bratkartoffeln. Medium. Englisch. Durchgebraten.

4. WUNDERBAR!

Ute: Das Schnitzel ist wirklich wunderbar!
The schnitzel is really wonderful!

Dieter: Und die Forelle . . . einfach vorzüglich! Bestellen wir noch eine Flasche Rotwein?
And the trout . . . simply excellent! Shall we order another bottle of red wine?

Frauke: Gute Idee!
Good idea!

Heinz: Und ich möchte noch ein Bier.
And I would like another beer.

Dieter: Herr Ober, noch eine Flasche Rotwein und ein Bier!
Waiter, another bottle of red wine and a beer!

Heinz: Und wie ist das Steak?
And how is the steak?

Frauke: Auch gut, aber ein bißchen zu durchgebraten.
Also good, but a little bit too well-done.

Waiter: Bitte sehr. Hat es geschmeckt?
Here you are. Have you enjoyed your meal?

Frauke: Oh ja, sehr gut! Vielen Dank!
Oh yes, very good! Thank you!

Waiter: Möchten Sie einen Kaffee oder eine
Nachspeise?
Would you like coffee or a dessert?

Dieter: Ja bitte! Vier Apfelstrudel mit Sahne und vier
Tassen Kaffee.
*Yes please! Four apple strudels with cream and four
cups of coffee.*

Frauke: Prost!
Cheers!

All: Prost! Zum Wohl!
Cheers! Good health!

Heinz: Ach übrigens, wie geht's Julia? Arbeitet sie
wieder?
By the way, how is Julia? Is she working again?

Dieter: Ja. Sie arbeitet bei Siemens in Berlin.
Yes. She is working for Siemens in Berlin.

Heinz: And was macht Florian?
And what is Florian doing?

Dieter: Er arbeitet bei Foto Fritz. Ich glaube, er ist
glücklich da. Und Elmar, was macht der?
*He is working for Foto Fritz. I think he is happy
there. And what about Elmar, what is he doing?*

Heinz: Der studiert Biologie in Hamburg. Er ist auch
glücklich. Ich glaube, er is verliebt.
*He is studying biology in Hamburg. He is happy
too. I think he is in love.*

4A. HOW IT SOUNDS
Wunderbar. Wirklich wunderbar. Vorzüglich. Einfach
vorzüglich. Das Schnitzel ist wirklich vorzüglich. Übrigens.
Ach übrigens, wie geht's Julia? Glücklich. Ich glaube. Ich
glaube, sie ist glücklich. Verliebt. Ich glaube, er ist verliebt.

5. WIR MÖCHTEN BEZAHLEN
Dieter: Herr Ober, wir möchten bezahlen!
Waiter, we would like to pay our bill!

Waiter: Getrennt oder zusammen?
Separately or together?

Dieter: Getrennt, bitte. Die Getränke, eine Zwiebelsuppe, eine Forelle blau, die Kaffees und die Apfelstrudel bezahle ich.
Separately, please. I will pay for the drinks, one onion soup, the trout, the coffees and the apple strudels.

Waiter: Das macht zusammen hundertsiebenundsechzig Mark achtzig.
That comes to 167.80 DM altogether.

Dieter: Hundertfünfundsiebzig bitte.
Here's 175. – he leaves 7.20 as a tip

Heinz: Und ich zahle die Wiener Schnitzel und zwei Tomatensuppen.
And I'm paying for the Wiener Schnitzel and two tomato soups.

Waiter: Das macht fünfundsechzig Mark.
That's 65 DM.

Heinz: Siebzig.
Here's 70.

Waiter: Danke!
Thank you!

Frauke: Und ich zahle den Rest: eine Zwiebelsuppe und ein Rumpsteak mit Kartoffel und Bohnen.
And I'll pay for the rest: an onion soup and a rump steak with potato and beans.

Waiter: Das sind zusammen achtundzwanzig Mark fünfzig.
That's 28.50 altogether.

Frauke: Fünfunddreißig Mark bitte.
Here's 35 DM.

Waiter: Vielen Dank, und schönen Abend noch!
Many thanks, and enjoy the rest of your evening!

 5A. HOW IT SOUNDS

Bezahlen. Zahlen. Wir möchten zahlen. Getrennt. Zusammen. Getrennt oder zusammen? Getränke. Ich zahle die Getränke. Apfelstrudel. Den Apfelstrudel bezahle ich. Ich bezahle den Apfelstrudel. Rest. Und ich zahle den Rest. Und den Rest zahle ich.

FOOD AND DRINK

As in any country, in Germany and Austria food and drink varies from north to south and east to west. Usually, meals are based on meat or fish and there is still only a limited choice of vegetarian dishes. However, if you go to a proper restaurant, and not to a **Kneipe** (*pub*) which basically serves fast food, you probably won't be disappointed.

As well as restaurants serving German food, you will find a wide variety of foreign restaurants – for instance, Italian, Greek, Turkish, Spanish. They are usually very good and often cheaper than the German ones.

If you like ice cream, you must visit one of the Italian "**Eiscafés**" – you will be delighted!

READING THE MENU

The menu can be daunting, if you let long words – like **Wiener Zwiebelrostbraten** – frighten you! Just divide the long compound names into single words and look them up in your dictionary. So: **Wien** – *Vienna*; **Zwiebel** – *onion*; **Rost** – *roast*; **Braten** – *roast joint*. For speed, just look up the last word in the compound name: it is usually the key.

WHAT TO TRY

In the north of Germany, try:
Sauerfleisch mit Bratkartoffeln (a main course)
Rote Grütze (a dessert)

And if you are brave enough, try **Eisbein und Sauerkraut**, a north German speciality, with a **Schnaps** afterwards to aid digestion. This dish is good, but very heavy.

In the south, don't miss:
Tafelspitz mit Apfelkren und Schnittlauchsauce (boiled beef, a main course)
Apfelstrudel mit Vanilleeis und Sahne (a dessert)

WINES

There are about ten wine-growing areas in Germany, producing mostly white wines. There is a lot more to German wine than Liebfraumilch! If you like dry (**trocken**) wine, try some Frankenwein. If you like it sweeter (**lieblich, süß**), you will probably be happy with Rheinhessen. If you are a real wine lover, why not go on a trip along one of Germany's beautiful **Weinstraßen** or along the river Mosel?

TIPPING

In restaurants, people usually leave around 10% of the bill as a tip, even though service is normally included. You can either leave the money on the table, or, as many people do, round the bill up to the next even number (see dialogue 5).

LANGUAGE NOTES

THE INFORMAL "YOU"

As already mentioned, "**Sie**" is the formal way of saying "you", whether you are speaking to one or to several people. The informal version, used among friends, is "**du**". But "**du**" is only used if you are speaking to one person; to a number of friends you would say "**ihr**" (with a small "i").

WE AND THEY – WIR, SIE

"We" is "**wir**" and "they" is "**sie**".

If you put these and "**ihr**" together with the singular pronouns you learnt in chapter 2 (page 22), you now know all the pronouns.

VERB ENDINGS

As you know, from chapter 2, verb endings change depending on the person doing the action. Here is the pattern of endings that all German verbs follow:

		trinken (*to drink*)	**bestellen** (*to order*)	**kommen** (*to come*)	**bezahlen** (*to pay*)
SINGULAR					
I	**ich**	trinke	bestelle	komme	bezahle
you (form.)	**Sie**	trinken	bestellen	kommen	bezahlen
you (inf.)	**du**	trinkst	bestellst	kommst	bezahlst
he/it	**er**				
she/it	**sie**	} trinkt	bestellt	kommt	bezahlt
it (neuter)	**es**				
PLURAL					
we	**wir**	trinken	bestellen	kommen	bezahlen
you (form.)	**Sie**	trinken	bestell	kommen	bezahlen
you (inf.)	**ihr**	trinkt	bestellt	kommt	bezahlt
they	**sie**	trinken	bestellen	kommen	bezahlen

There are some verbs in German, called <u>strong verbs</u>, which not only change their endings in this way, but also change in another way in the "**du**" and "**er/sie/es**" forms. Here are two examples:

	nehmen (*to take*)	**essen** (*to eat*)
ich	nehme	esse
Sie	nehmen	essen
du	**nimmst**	**ißt**
er/sie/es	**nimmt**	**ißt**
wir	nehmen	essen
Sie	nehmen	essen
ihr	nehmt	**eßt**
sie	nehmen	essen

TO HAVE AND TO BE

Finally, here are the complete endings of the two important irregular verbs, "to have" – "haben" and "to be" – "sein".

	haben	**sein**
ich	habe	bin
Sie	haben	sind
du	hast	bist
er/sie/es	hat	ist
wir	haben	sind
Sie	haben	sind
ihr	habt	seid
sie	haben	sind

GOOD NEWS!

You have now learned all the verb endings for the present tense – and you will find that this can take you a long way. For instance, in the following sentences, the present tense covers several meanings:

Ich trinke Bier   *I drink beer (I like it)*
Ich trinke ein Bier *I'm drinking a beer (at the moment)*
Ich trinke ein Bier *I'll have a beer*

WORD ORDER

In English, the subject always goes in front of the verb. But German word order is different: the subject can go in front of the verb or after it. The verb, however, always comes <u>in the second position</u> in a simple sentence. For example:

Ich möchte Zwiebelsuppe. (*I would like onion soup.*)
Zwiebelsuppe möchte ich. (*I would like onion soup.*)

Als Hauptgericht nehme ich Forelle blau. (*As main course, I'll have trout.*)
Ich nehme als Hauptgericht Forelle blau. (*I'll have trout as main course.*)

Danach nimmt Ute ein Rumpsteak. (*Afterwards, Ute will have a rumpsteak.*)

Ute nimmt danach ein Rumpsteak. (*Ute will have a rumpsteak afterwards.*)

Zusammen macht das 128.50 DM. (*Together that makes 128.50 DM.*)

Das macht zusammen 128.50 DM. (*That makes 128.50 DM altogether.*)

As you can see in the first example, even the object can come before the subject, provided that the verb is in the second position of the sentence. This will probably seem very unfamiliar to you, but do not worry: when you speak yourself, you can always put the subject first. You only need to understand that people talking to you might have built their sentences the other way.

ER OR DER?

In spoken language you may hear people use "**der**" and "**die**" in the following way:

Und Dieter? Was macht der? (*And what is Dieter doing?*)
Und Waltraud? Was macht die? (*And what is Waltraud doing?*)

If these questions were written they would be:

Und Dieter? Was macht er?
Und Waltraud? Was macht sie?

YOUR TURN

1. BOOK A TABLE!

Write down your part of the following telephone conversation and then check with the key on page 72. Also, practise saying your part, with the tape if possible.

Reception: Restaurant Wiechmann. Guten Tag!
You: (Introduce yourself and say that you would like to book a table for tonight.)
Reception: Für wieviele Personen?
You: (For six.)

Reception: Um wieviel Uhr kommen Sie?
You: (At 10 o'clock.)
Reception: Und wie ist Ihr Name nochmal bitte?
You: (Give your name.)
Reception: Und Ihre Telefonnummer?
You: (Give your telephone number.)
Reception: Der Tisch ist für Sie reserviert. Vielen Dank!
You: (Say thank you and goodbye.)

2. READ THE MENU!

Read the German menu on the following page and match the numbered items with the correct English translation:
a) Warm apple strudel with cream
b) Red berry pudding with vanilla sauce
c) Trout with salted potatoes and lettuce
d) Pork escalope with rice and salad
e) Onion soup with cheese
f) Smoked trout with horseradish and cream
g) Chicken soup with noodles
h) Rump steak with baked potato, herb butter and green beans
i) Honey melon with Parma ham.
j) Rump steak with onion sauce, fried potatoes and salad
k) Herring in cream sauce
l) Tomato soup
m) Veal escalope in breadcrumbs with chips and vegetables
n) North Sea plaice with potato salad and tartar sauce
o) Mixed ice cream with cream

Restaurant Harenberger Hof

Geöffnet Dienstag–Samstag von 16.00 – 1.00 Uhr
Montags – Ruhetag

SPEISEKARTE

VORSPEISEN

1 Geräucherte Forelle mit Merettichsahne 12.20 DM
2 Honigmelone mit Parmaschinken 14.00 DM
3 Hering in Sahnesauce 10.50 DM

SUPPEN

4 Hühnersuppe mit Nudeln 5.00 DM
5 Tomatensuppe 5.00 DM
6 Zwiebelsuppe mit Käse 5.50 DM

HAUPTGERICHTE

7 Wiener Schnitzel mit Pommes frites und Gemüse 15.00 DM
8 Rumpsteak mit gebackener Kartoffel, Kräuterbutter und grünen Bohnen
22.50 DM
9 Zigeunerschnitzel mit Reis und Salat 14.30 DM
10 Wiener Zwiebelrostbraten mit Bratkartoffeln und Salat 16.00 DM
11 Forelle blau mit Salzkartoffeln und Blattsalat 15.50 DM
12 Nordseescholle mit Kartoffelsalat und Remoladensauce 14.00 DM

NACHSPEISEN

13 Rote Grütze mit Vanillesauce 4.50 DM
14 Gemischtes Eis mit Sahne 4.00 DM
15 Warmer Apfelstrudel mit Sahne 4.50 DM

3. WHAT'S THE RIGHT WORD ORDER?

Put these words in the right order, to make sense. There are at least two correct answers in each case.

a) ich die Tomatensuppe als Vorspeise möchte

b) möchte mit Kräuterbutter und Bohnen ein Rumpsteak ich

c) erst ich ein Zwiebelsuppe und dann esse ein Wiener Schnitzel

4. FILL IN THE GAPS!

Waiter: Bitteschön!

You: [*Choose your starter*] Ich hätte gern al_ Vor___se _____
_____. [*Choose your main course*] Dann
neh__ ich _____.

Waiter: Und was möchten Sie trinken?

You: [*Your choice of drink*]_____, b____.

Waiter: Danke schön!

WORD LIST

der Apfelsaft (-säfte)	apple juice
der Apfelstrudel	apple strudel
die Biologie	biology
die Bohne (-n)	bean
die Forelle (-n)	trout
das Gemüse	vegetable
das Getränk (-e)	drink
das Glas (Gläser)	glass
das Hauptgericht (-e)	main course
der Hauswein	house wine
der Hering (-e)	herring
die Hühnersuppe	chicken soup
der Kaffee (-s)	coffee
das Kännchen	little pot
die Karte (-n)	menu
die Kartoffel (-n)	potato
die Melone (-n)	melon
das Mineralwasser	mineral water
die Nachspeise (-n)	dessert
die Nudel (-n)	noodle
die Person (-en)	person
der Reis	rice
der Rest (-e)	rest
das Rumpsteak (-s)	rump steak
die Sahne	cream
der Salat	salad
die Salzkartoffeln	salt potatoes
die Sauce Or die Soße	sauce
der Schinken	ham

das Schnitzel	fillet, cutlet
die Scholle (-n)	plaice
die Speisekarte (-n)	menu
das Steak (-s)	steak
die Suppe (-n)	soup
die Tasse (-n)	cup
der Tee (-s)	tea
der Tisch (-e)	table
die Tomatensuppe (-n)	tomato soup
die Uhr (-en)	hour
die Vorspeise (-n)	starter
die Zwiebel (-n)	onion
bestellen	to order
essen	to eat
glauben	to believe, to think
schmecken	to taste
studieren	to study
trinken	to drink
blau	blue
danach	afterwards
durchgebraten	well-done (of meat)
ein bißchen	a little
einfach	simple, simply
englisch	rare (of meat)
gebacken	baked
getrennt	separated, separately
glücklich	happy
groß	big, large
grün	green
klein	small
lecker	delicious
medium	medium
rot	red
trocken	dry
um	around, at
verliebt	in love
vorzüglich	excellent
warum?	why?
weiß	white
wieder	again
wirklich	really, truly
wunderbar	wonderful, lovely
zuerst	first (of all)
zweimal	twice

USEFUL EXPRESSIONS

Getrennt oder zusammen?	Together or separately?
Gute Idee!	Good idea!
Hat es geschmeckt?	Did you enjoy your meal?
Herr Ober!	Waiter! (to call his attention)
Ich möchte lieber . . .	I would prefer . . .
Noch { **einen . . .** **eine . . .** **ein . . .**	Another . . .
Prost!	Cheers!
Schönen Abend!	Have a good evening!
Übrigens . . .	By the way, . . .
Um wieviel Uhr?	At what time?
Wir hätten gern . . .	We would like . . .
Zum Wohl!	Good health!

KEY

1. BOOK A TABLE!
Guten Tag! Mein Name ist [*your name*]. Ich möchte einen Tisch für heute abend reservieren.
Für sechs (Personen).
Um Zehn Uhr.
Mein Name ist [*your name*].
Meine Telefonnummer ist [*your telephone number*].
Vielen Dank. Auf Wiederhören!

2. READ THE MENU!
1 f; 2 i; 3 k; 4 g; 5 l; 6 e; 7 m; 8 h; 9 d; 10 j; 11 c; 12 n; 13 b; 14 o; 15 a.

3. WHAT'S THE RIGHT WORD ORDER?
a) Ich möchte als Vorspeise die Tomatensuppe. OR
   Als Vorspeise möchte ich die Tomatensuppe.
b) Ich möchte ein Rumpsteak mit Kräuterbutter und Bohnen. OR
   Ein Rumpsteak möchte ich mit Kräuterbutter und Bohnen.
c) Ich esse erst eine Zwiebelsuppe und dann ein Wiener Schnitzel.
OR   Erst esse ich eine Zwiebelsuppe und dann ein Wiener Schnitzel.

4. FILL IN THE GAPS!
Ich hätte gern als Vorspeise [*whatever you fancy*].
Dann nehme ich [*your choice!*]
[*your choice of drink*], bitte!

6 Time and Travel

1. WIE SPÄT IST ES?

Dieter: Wie spät ist es?
What time is it?

Frauke: Keine Ahnung!
No idea!

Dieter: Ich rufe mal die Zeitansage an. Wie ist die Telefonnummer?
I'll call the speaking clock. What's the number?

Frauke: Null- eins- eins- neun- neun.
01199.

Clock: Beim nächsten Ton ist es elf Uhr, zehn Minuten und zwanzig Sekunden – (tüt) – beim nächsten Ton ist es elf Uhr, zehn Minuten und dreißig Sekunden – (tüt) – beim nächsten Ton . . .
At the next stroke, it will be 11 hours, 10 minutes and 20 seconds – beep – at the next stroke, it will be 11 hours, 10 minutes and 30 seconds – beep – at the next stroke . . .

73

Frauke: Wie spät ist es?
What is the time?

Dieter: Es ist zehn nach elf.
It's 10 past 11.

1A. HOW IT SOUNDS

Wie spät? Wie spät ist es? 11 Uhr 10. 11 Uhr 11. 11 Uhr 22. 22 Uhr 13. 1 Uhr 34. 23 Uhr 12. 06 Uhr 03. 10 nach 11. 11 nach 11.

2. UM WIEVIEL UHR FÄHRT DER NÄCHSTE ZUG NACH BERLIN?

Anette: Entschuldigung! Um wieviel Uhr fährt der nächste Zug nach Berlin?
Excuse me! What time is the next train to Berlin?

Ticket office: Um elf Uhr zwei.
At 11.02.

Anette: Ist das ein Intercity oder ein D-Zug?
Is that an intercity or a slower train?

Ticket office: Ein Intercity. Er kommt um fünfzehn Uhr dreißig in Berlin am Bahnhof Zoo an.
An intercity. It arrives at Berlin Zoo station at 15.30

Anette: Gut. Ich möchte eine Fahrkarte zweiter Klasse.
Right. I would like one second-class ticket.

Ticket office: Einfach oder hin und zurück?
Single or return?

Anette: Hin und zurück bitte.
Return please.

Ticket office: Das macht hundertzwei Mark fünfzig.
That's 102.50 Deutschmarks.

Anette: Hat der Zug einen Speisewagen?
Has the train got a restaurant car?

Ticket office: Ja, natürlich.
Yes, of course.

Anette: Und von wo fährt der Zug ab?
And where does the train leave from?

Ticket office: Von Gleis zwölf.
From platform 12.

Anette: Danke.
Thank you.

2A. HOW IT SOUNDS

Zug. Der nächste Zug. Um wieviel Uhr fährt der nächste Zug?
Entschuldigung! Um wieviel Uhr fährt der nächste Zug nach
Berlin? Bahnhof. Bahnhof Zoo. Der Zug kommt um zwei Uhr
am Bahnhof Zoo an. Einfach. Einfach oder hin und zurück?
Natürlich. Ja, natürlich.

3. HALLO! HIER IST ANETTE!

Ute: Berg!

Berg! – she answers her phone by announcing her surname.

Anette: Hallo, Ute! Hier ist Anette. Na, wie geht's?

Hello, Ute! This is Anette. So how are you?

Ute: Gut, und dir?

Fine. And you?

Anette: Auch gut. Du, ich komme heute um halb vier
am Bahnhof Zoo an. Holst du mich ab?

*Also fine. Listen, I am arriving at Berlin Zoo today
at 3.30. Can you pick me up?*

Ute: Klar! Kommen Jörg und Valentin auch mit?

Sure! Are Jörg and Valentin coming with you?

Anette: Valentin kommt mit, aber Jörg bleibt noch eine
Woche in Hannover.

*Valentin's coming too, but Jörg is staying in
Hanover for another week.*

Ute: Gut. Ich bin um halb vier da. Bis dann. Tschüß!

OK. I'll be there at 3.30. Until then, bye!

Anette: Tschüß!

Bye!

3A. HOW IT SOUNDS

Hallo! Hallo! Hier ist Anette. Na, wie geht's? Gut. Auch gut.
Klar! Kommen Jörg und Valentin mit? Woche. Eine Woche.
Jörg bleibt noch eine Woche in Hannover. Tschüß! Tschüß, bis
dann!

4. DER ZUG HAT VERSPÄTUNG

Anette: Entschuldigung! Wie spät ist es?
Excuse me! What is the time?

Guard: Gleich halb drei. Der Zug hat eine Stunde fünfzehn Minuten Verspätung.
Almost half past two. The train is one hour 15 minutes late.

Anette: Gibt es hier ein Zugtelefon?
Is there a telephone on this train?

Guard: Ja, in der ersten Klasse.
Yes, in the first-class section.

Anette: Vielen Dank!
Thank you!

Ute: Berg!
Berg! – answering the telephone

Anette: Hallo, Ute! Hier ist Anette. Du, der Zug hat eine Stunde fünfzehn Minuten Verspätung. Wir sind also erst um viertel vor fünf in Berlin.
Hello, Ute! This is Anette. The train is delayed by an hour and fifteen minutes. So we won't be in Berlin until a quarter to five.

Ute: OK. Dann komme ich um viertel vor fünf. Bis dann!
OK. Then I will come at a quarter to five. Till then!

Anette: Bis dann!
See you then!

4A. HOW IT SOUNDS

Verspätung. Der Zug hat 15 Minuten Verspätung. Gibt es. Gibt es hier ein Telefon? Gibt es hier ein Zugtelefon? Um viertel vor vier. Um viertel nach vier. Um viertel vor fünf. Um viertel nach fünf.

5. GIBT ES NOCH FLÜGE NACH NEW YORK?

Dieter: Gibt es am ersten April noch Flüge nach New York?
Are there flights to New York still available for the 1st April?

Information: Von Berlin Tempelhof?
From Berlin Tempelhof?
Dieter: Nein. Von Berlin Tegel, bitte.
No. From Berlin Tegel, please.
Information: Moment, bitte . . . Fliegen Sie erster Klasse, business- oder Tourist-class?
One moment please . . . Are you flying first-class, business- or tourist-class?
Dieter: Tourist-class, bitte.
Tourist-class, please.
Information: Tut mir leid, aber da haben wir nichts mehr.
I am sorry, but we don't have any seats left.
Dieter: Und am zweiten April?
And for 2nd April?
Information: Am zweiten April gibt es noch Plätze. Die Maschine geht um zehn nach elf ab Berlin Tegel.
On 2nd April there are seats left. The plane leaves Berlin Tegel at 10 past 11.
Dieter: Um zehn nach elf? Das ist ein bißchen früh. Gibt es noch einen anderen Flug?
At 10 past 11? That is rather early. Is there another flight after that?
Information: Nein. Tut mir leid. Die Maschine um viёrzehn Uhr fünfundvierzig ist total ausgebucht.
No. I'm sorry. The 14.45 plane is completely booked.
Dieter: OK. Ich nehme den Flug um elf Uhr zehn. Wann komme ich in New York an?
OK. I'll take the 11.10 flight. When will I arrive in New York?
Information: Um sechszehn Uhr zehn Ortszeit.
At 16.10 local time.
Dieter: Gut.
Right.

5A. HOW IT SOUNDS

Flug. Flüge. Tut mir leid. Das tut mir leid. Maschine. Die Maschine geht um 11.10 Uhr ab Tegel. Ein bißchen. Ein bißchen zu früh. Ausgebucht. Total ausgebucht. Ortszeit. Die Maschine kommt um 16.10 Uhr Ortszeit in New York an.

INFORMATION

TRAINS

If you don't have a car but want to travel around Germany, trains are probably the most convenient means of transport. Different types of train travel at different speeds and it is worth knowing which are the quicker ones.

The ICE is the fastest train in Europe. It takes only a few hours from Hamburg to Frankfurt. It is first- and second-class only and you have to pay a supplement.
The IC is a fast train. You have to pay a supplement on this too.
The D-Zug is a little slower than the IC and there is no supplement to pay.
The E-Zug is considerably slower; it stops everywhere! Of course, there is no supplement to pay.

Many trains have a luggage compartment (**Gepäckwagen**), if you want to take a bicycle or any other heavy luggage.
   If you have a car, but want a rest from driving, you can take it on the **Autoreisezug**.

BUYING YOUR TICKET

Usually you will get a seat on most trains, but if you want to be sure, you can make a reservation (**Reservierung**) at a railway station or a travel agent's, at least three days before your journey.
   If you travel with your family or with a group of people, you can get a price reduction. People under 18 and pensioners pay less than other passengers. You can find out about this at the station or the travel agent's.

HITCHING

Travelling by train is rather expensive and unfortunately there are no coaches linking the bigger cities. If you cannot afford the train fare, you might try telephoning one of the many hitching agencies (**Mitfahrzentralen**). You can find them in all big towns in Germany and because many people use this form of transport today, it is becoming increasingly efficient. You meet the person who is offering a lift at the agency, pay a minimal set fee to the agent, and then share the petrol costs with the driver of the car. And you will be fully insured.

If you have a car and find driving alone rather boring or expensive, or if you simply want to practise your German, you could phone one of the hitching agencies and offer a lift yourself.

LANGUAGE NOTES

TELLING THE TIME

There are two ways of telling the time in German, the "official" way and the "informal" way. You need to understand both, but you may find the official way easier for telling the time yourself.

To ask what the time is, say **"Wie spät ist es?"**

The answer might be:

Es ist ein Uhr

Es ist ein Uhr zwei (Minuten)   01.02

Es ist zehn Uhr fünf (Minuten)

Es ist elf Uhr fünfzehn   11.15

Es ist elf Uhr fünfundvierzig

Es ist zwölf Uhr zweiundzwanzig   12.22

Es ist sechzehn Uhr vierundfünfzig – OR
vier Uhr vierundfünfzig   16.54

Es ist achtzehn Uhr vierunddreißig – OR sechs Uhr vierunddreißig

18.34

Es ist zweiundzwanzig Uhr dreißig – OR zehn Uhr dreißig

This is the official way of telling the time, as used at railway stations, airports, by the "speaking clock" on the telephone. Of course, when you use this way of telling the time yourself, you don't have to use the 24-hour clock!

The informal way of telling the time is like this:

Es ist eins – OR Es ist ein Uhr

Es ist fünf nach eins

01.05

Es ist fünf vor eins

Es ist zehn nach vier

16.10

Es ist zehn vor vier

Es ist viertel nach fünf

17.15

Es ist halb neun

Es ist halb fünf

04.30

Es ist zehn nach halb fünf

Es ist zehn vor halb fünf

04.20

Es ist fünf nach halb acht

Es ist fünf vor halb acht

07.25

As you see, the informal way is a bit more complicated! If you find it too difficult to use, you can always use the "official" way. But you need to understand the informal way. One important thing to remember is that the Germans don't think of 8.30, for instance, as "half past" the hour, but as "half to" the next hour.

VERBS WITH TWO PARTS

As you know, the verb in a German sentence always comes second (except in questions, where it comes first). Some verbs have two parts, which are separable. For instance, "**ankommen**", which means *"to arrive"*, or "**mitkommen**", which means *"to come with"* or *"to accompany"*. The "**an**" or the "**mit**" part is called the prefix, and when such a verb is used in a sentence the prefix separates and goes to the end of that sentence:

Der Zug **kommt** um 15.30 Uhr in Berlin **an**.
Wo **fährt** der Zug **ab**?
Valentin **kommt** auch **mit**.
Du **holst** mich **ab**.

Kommt Valentin auch **mit**?
Holst du mich um 15.30 Uhr **ab**?
Fährt der Zug von Gleis 12 **ab**?

FAHREN

"**Fahren**" (*to travel, to go*) is a strong verb (see page 65). In the "**du**" and "**er/sie/es**" forms, "**a**" changes to "**ä**":

ich fahre	wir fahren
Sie fahren	Sie fahren
du **fährst**	ihr fahrt
er/sie/es **fährt**	sie fahren

YOUR TURN

1. WIE SPÄT IST ES?
Write down how you would say the following, in the official way:
a) 10.05 Uhr _____
b) 17.30 Uhr _____
c) 12.55 Uhr _____
d) 00.05 Uhr _____
e) 22.30 Uhr _____
f) 11.25 Uhr _____

2. THE SPEAKING CLOCK
Listen to the speaking clock on the tape, and write down the times it gives. Check your answers with the key on page 86.

3. WIEVIEL UHR?
Write down how you would say the times in exercise 1, in the informal way. Check your answers with the key on page 86.

4. TRAIN TIMES
Listen to the conversation on the tape and write down the three times you will hear there. Check your answers with the key on page 86.

5. FILL IN THE GAPS!
Fill in the gaps in the following sentences, using these words:

fährt ab   komme an   kommen an   kommt an

a) Um wieviel Uhr _____ der Zug nach Hannover __?
b) Der Zug _____ um 10 Uhr in Hannover __.
c) Wann _____ ich in Hannover __?
d) Sie _____ um 14 Uhr in Hannover __.

holst ab   kommt an   kommt mit   hole ab

e) Anette _____ heute um 14 Uhr in Berlin __.
f) _____ du sie __?

g) Klar _____ ich sie __.

h) _____ Valentin auch __?

Check your answers with the key on page 86.

6. AT THE TRAVEL AGENT'S

Write down your parts of the conversation, check them with the key on page 86, and practise speaking them, with the tape if you can.

You: (Say hello and ask if there are still flights available to London on 1st May.)

Agent: Moment, bitte . . . Ja. Fliegen Sie tourist- oder business-class?

You: (Business please. Ask when the flights are leaving.)

Agent: Eine Maschine geht um 7.05 Uhr und eine geht um 18.30 Uhr ab Hannover.

You: (Say you will take the flight at 18.30. Ask what time you will arrive in London.)

Agent: Um 19.00 Uhr Ortszeit.

You: (Say OK and thank you.)

7. QUESTIONS AND ANSWERS

Find the two possible answers for the following five questions:

1. Wie spät ist es?
2. Um wieviel Uhr fährt der Zug?
3. Wie geht's?
4. Ist das ein Intercity?
5. Wieviel kostet das?

a) Nein, das ist ein D-Zug.
b) Ja, das ist ein Intercity.
c) Es ist 10 nach 11.
d) Das macht 102.50 DM.
e) Keine Ahnung!
f) Um 14.30 Uhr.
g) Gut. Und dir?
h) Gut. Und Ihnen?
i) Das kostet 50 DM.
j) Der Zug fährt um 14.30 Uhr ab Gleis 12.

WORD LIST

die Ahnung (-en)	idea
der Bahnhof (-höfe)	station
die Fahrkarte (-n)	ticket
der Fluzg (Flüge)	flight
das Gepäck (-e)	luggage
das Gleis (-e)	platform
die Klasse (-n)	class
die Maschine (-n)	machine, aeroplane
die Minute (-n)	minute
der Ort (-e)	place
die Ortszeit	local time
der Platz (Plätze)	place, seat
die Sekunde (-n)	second
der Speisewagen	restaurant car
die Stunde (-n)	hour
das Telefon (-s)	telephone
der Ton (Töne)	beep, tone, sound
die Verspätung	delay
der Wagen	carriage (train)
die Woche (-n)	week
die Zeit	time
die Zeitansage	speaking clock
der Zug (Züge)	train
abfahren	to leave
abholen	to fetch
ankommen	to arrive
anrufen	to call
bleiben	to stay
fahren	to travel
fliegen	to fly
mitkommen	to accompany
ab	away, from
an	to
ausgebucht	booked up
ander	other
einfach	single (ticket)
früh	early
gleich	immediately
hin	there
kein	no
mehr	more
mit	with, by

nach	after
nächst	next
nichts mehr	nothing more
spät	late
total	completely
vor	before
zurück	back, back again

USEFUL EXPRESSIONS

Bis dann	Until then/See you soon!
Einfach oder hin und zurück?	Single or return?
Es gibt . . .	There is . . .
Gibt es . . . ?	Is there . . . ?
Keine Ahnung!	No idea!
Klar!	Sure!/Of course!
Naturlich!	Naturally!/Of course!
Tschüß!	Bye!
Um wieviel Uhr?	When?/At what time?
Wie spät ist es?	What's the time?

1. WIE SPÄT IST ES?

a) zehn Uhr fünf; b) siebzehn Uhr dreißig; c) zwölf Uhr fünfundfünfzig; d) null Uhr fünf; e) zweiundzwanzig Uhr dreißig; f) elf Uhr fünfundzwanzig.

2. THE SPEAKING CLOCK

Beim nächsten Ton ist es 23 Uhr, 17 Minuten und 10 Sekunden.
Beim nächsten Ton ist es 14 Uhr, 2 Minuten und 30 Sekunden.
Beim nächsten Ton ist es 12 Uhr, 50 Minuten und 40 Sekunden.

3. WIEVIEL UHR?

a) fünf nach zehn; b) halb sechs; c) fünf vor eins; d) fünf nach zwölf; e) halb elf; f) fünf vor halb zwölf.

4. TRAIN TIMES

Entschuldigen Sie bitte! Wie spät ist es?
Es ist zehn nach acht. (8.10).
Und um wieviel Uhr fährt der Zug nach Hannover?
Um viertel vor neun. (8.45).
Und um wieviel Uhr commet der Zug in Hannover an?
Um halb eins. (12.30).

5. FILL IN THE GAPS!

a) fährt . . . ab; b) kommt . . . an; c) komme . . . an; d) kommen an; e) kommt . . . an; f) Holst . . . ab; g) hole . . . ab; h) Kommt . . . mit.

6. AT THE TRAVEL AGENT'S

Hallo! Gibt es am ersten Mai noch Flüge nach London?
Business-class bitte. Um wieviel Uhr gehen die Flüge?
Ich nehme den Flug um 18.30 Uhr. Um wieviel Uhr komme ich in London an?
Gut. Vielen Dank!

7. QUESTIONS AND ANSWERS

1 c, 1 e; 2 f, 2 j, 2 e; 3 g, 3 h, 3 e; 4 a, 4 b, 4 e; 5 d, 5 i, 5 e.

7 Getting About

1. ICH SUCHE DAS SCHLOSS CHARLOTTENBURG

Visitor: Entschuldigen Sie bitte! Ich suche das Schloß Charlottenburg.
Excuse me! I'm looking for Charlottenburg Palace.

Passer-by: Mhm. Gehen Sie hier geradeaus, die Sophie Charlottenstraße entlang.
Mhm. Go straight along the Sophie Charlottenstraße.

Visitor: Hier geradeaus . . .
Straight on here . . .

Passer-by: Ja, und dann nach rechts in die Klausenerstraße und dann ist links das Schloß Charlottenburg.
Yes, and then turn right into Klausenerstraße and Charlottenburg Palace is on the left.

Visitor: Also, ich gehe erst hier geradeaus die Sophie Charlottenstraße entlang, dann rechts in die Klausenerstraße and dann nach links. Da ist das Schloß Charlottenburg. Stimmt das?
So, first I go from here straight along the Sophie Charlottenstraße, then right into Klausenerstraße and then left. Is that right?

Passer-by: Ja, genau.
Yes, exactly.

1A. HOW IT SOUNDS
Entschuldigen Sie! Entschuldigen Sie bitte! Ich suche. Schloß Charlottenburg. Ich suche das Schloß Charlottenburg. Nach rechts. Nach links. Nach rechts and dann nach links.

2. ZUM HOTEL BRANDENBURGER TOR, BITTE!
Passenger: Guten Tag! Zum Hotel Brandenburger Tor, bitte.
Good morning/afternoon! To the Brandenburger Tor hotel please.

Driver: OK . . . Hier ist das Hotel.
OK . . . Here's the hotel.

Passenger: Warten Sie bitte einen Moment. Ich bin sofort wieder zurück.
Please wait a moment. I'll be right back.

Driver: OK.
OK.

Passenger: Und jetzt fahren Sie mich bitte zur Stadthalle.
And now please drive me to the town hall.

Driver: Stadthalle!
Here's the town hall.

Passenger: Moment bitte. Ich bin gleich wieder zurück . . .
Und jetzt möchte ich zu den Thermen.
Wait a moment please. I'll be right back again . . .
And now I would like to go to the baths.

Driver: Alles klar . . . Und jetzt?
All right . . . And now?

Passenger: Jetzt fahren Sie mich bitte zurück zum Hotel
Brandenburger Tor.
Now please drive me back to the Brandenburger Tor
hotel.

Driver: Brandenburger Tor!
Here's the Brandenburger Tor!

Passenger: Vielen Dank! Was macht das?
Many thanks! How much is that?

Driver: Zweiundachtzig Mark fünfzig.
82.50 Deutschmarks.

Passenger: Stimmt so.
That's fine – giving him 90, implying he can keep
the change.

Driver: Danke schön!
Thank you very much!

2A. HOW IT SOUNDS

Zum. Zum Hotel. Zurück. Ich bin sofort wieder zurück. Zur
Stadthalle. Fahren Sie! Fahren Sie mich bitte zur Stadthalle!
Jetzt. Und jetzt möchte ich zu den Thermen. Zusammen. Was
macht das zusammen?

3. OH, MEIN GOTT!

Anette: Oh, mein Gott! Wo sind wir?
Oh, my God! Where are we?

Valentin: Keine Ahnung!
No idea!

Anette: Entschuldigung! Wie kommen wir von hier zur
Boddinstraße?
Excuse me! How do we get from here to
Boddinstraße? [– a station on the Berlin metro]

Passenger: Mhm. Wir sind hier – in Marienfelde. Fahren Sie mit der Linie zwei zurück bis zur Yorkstraße. Fahren Sie dann mit der Linie sieben in Richtung Rudow bis zum Hermannplatz. Ich glaube, das sind ungefähr fünf Stationen. Fahren Sie dann mit der Linie acht Richtung Leinestraße bis zur Boddinstraße.

Mhm. We are here – in Marienfelde. Take the number 2 train back to Yorkstraße. Then take the number 7 towards Rudow and get off at Hermannplatz. I think it's about 5 stations. Then take the number 8 towards Leinestraße, to Boddinstraße.

Anette: Wie bitte?

Pardon?

Passenger: Fahren Sie vom Hermannplatz mit der Linie acht Richtung Leinestraße bis zur Boddinstraße. Das ist die nächste Station.

From Hermannplatz take the number 8 towards Leinestraße, to Boddinstraße. It's the next stop.

Anette/Valentin: Vielen Dank!

Thank you!

3A. HOW IT SOUNDS

Gott. Oh, mein Gott! Oh mein Gott! Wo sind wir? Wie kommen wir zur Boddinstraße? Ich glaube. Ich glaube, das sind fünf Stationen. Die nächste Station. Das ist die nächste Station.

4. WO KANN MAN HIER GELD WECHSELN?

Visitor: Entschuldigung! Wo kann man hier Geld wechseln?

Excuse me! Where can you change money here?

Passer-by: Gehen Sie zum Ernst Reuter Platz. Da ist eine Bank.

Go to Ernst Reuter Platz. There is a bank there.

Visitor: Und wo kann man hier einkaufen?

And where can you go shopping?

Passer-by: Was möchten Sie denn einkaufen?
What would you like to buy?

Visitor: Souvenirs.
Souvenirs.

Passer-by: Keine Ahnung!
I've no idea!

Visitor: OK. Danke . . . Ach, und wo kann man hier gut essen?
OK. Thank you . . . Oh, and where can you get a good meal?

Passer-by: Gehen Sie zur Touristenzentrale. Ich hab' keine Ahnung!
Go to the tourist office. I have no idea!

Visitor: Und wo ist eine Touristenzentrale?
And where is there a tourist office?

Passer-by: Das weiß ich auch nicht. Tut mir leid.
I don't know that either. I am sorry.

4A. HOW IT SOUNDS

Wechseln. Geld wechseln. Entshuldigung! Entschuldigung, wo kann man hier Geld wechseln? Gehen Sie. Gehen Sie zum Ernst Reuter Platz. Ich weiß nicht. Ich weiß auch nicht. Das weiß ich auch nicht.

5. HABEN SIE INFORMATION ÜBER BERLIN?

Visitor: Guten Tag! Haben Sie Information über Berlin?
Good morning/afternoon! Do you have information about Berlin?

Office: Ja, natürlich! Was möchten Sie wissen?
. *Yes, of course! What would you like to know?*

Visitor: Wir suchen ein gutes Restaurant.
We're looking for a good restaurant.

Office: Möchten Sie deutsch, italienisch, türkisch, griechisch oder spanisch essen?
Would you like to eat German, Italian, Turkish, Greek or Spanish?

Visitor: Können Sie etwas empfehlen?
Can you recommend something?

Office: Ja. Gehen Sie ins Restaurant Wiechmann. Das
ist sehr, sehr gut. Aber nicht so billig.
*Yes. Go to the Restaurant Wiechmann. It is very,
very good. But not that cheap.*

Visitor: Und wo ist das?
And where is that?

Office: Spiechernstraße.
Spiechernstraße.

Visitor: Gut! Und wo kann man hier einkaufen?
Good! And where can one go shopping here?

Office: Gehen Sie ins Kaufhaus des Westens. Das ist am
Kurfürsten Damm. Da finden Sie alles.
*Go to the Kaufhaus des Westens. It's on the
Kurfürsten Damm. You'll find everything there.*

Visitor: Gut! Vielen Dank!
Great! Thank you!

5A. HOW IT SOUNDS
Information. Haben Sie Information über Berlin? Natürlich. Ja,
natürlich. Wissen. Was möchten Sie wissen? Empfehlen.
Können Sie etwas empfehlen?

INFORMATION

PUBLIC TRANSPORT
You will find the buses, trams and underground systems in
Germany very reliable.

You can buy different types of tickets: a single ticket, ten at
once, a one-week or one-month travel card, or – in Berlin – a
transferable green card. Tickets are available from newsagents
at rail and underground stations, at bus and tram stops, and
on the buses or trams.

If you buy a single ticket or ten in a row, you must get your
ticket stamped when you use it; otherwise it is not valid and
fines for travelling without a valid ticket are huge. To get your
ticket stamped, you must insert it in one of the machines
provided at all stations, on buses and on trams.

TOURIST INFORMATION

Tourist information offices (**Fremdenverkehrsbüros** or **Touristenzentralen**) provide information on accommodation, local restaurants, shopping facilities, transport, places of interest, etc, and you can ask them for maps, too. All this is free of charge.

You will find the tourist information office near the main station or in the town centre.

LANGUAGE NOTES

THE DATIVE CASE

In chapter 4 (page 48) you learnt about the nominative and accusative cases (subjects and objects). The endings of the definite and indefinite articles and the forms of the pronouns change, according to the case. The dialogues in this chapter have introduced one further case – the dative. It is used after words like "**mit**", "**zu**" and "**von**".

Here are the different forms of the articles and pronouns:

	nominative	accusative	dative
masculine	**der**	**den**	**dem**
feminine	**die**	**die**	**der**
neuter	**das**	**das**	**dem**
plural (all genders)	**die**	**die**	**den**
masculine	**ein**	**einen**	**einem**
feminine	**eine**	**eine**	**einer**
neuter	**ein**	**ein**	**einem**
I, me, to me	**ich**	**mich**	**mir**
you (informal)	**du**	**dich**	**dir**
you (formal)	**Sie**	**Sie**	**Ihnen**
he/it, him, to him	**er**	**ihn**	**ihm**
she/it, her, to her	**sie**	**sie**	**ihr**
it (neuter)	**es**	**es**	**ihm**
we, us, to us	**wir**	**uns**	**uns**
you (informal)	**ihr**	**euch**	**euch**
they, them, to them	**sie**	**sie**	**ihnen**

THE DATIVE WITH "MIT"

"**Mit**" means "*with*", but is also used where the English might say "*by*" or "*on*":

Ich komme **mit einem** Freund. (*I'm coming with a friend.*)
Ich fahre **mit dem** Bus. (*I'm going by bus.*)
Ich fahre **mit der** Linie 8. (*I'm going by route 8.*)
Ich fahre **mit dem** Auto. (*I'm going by car.*)
Ich fahre **mit den** U-Bahnlinien 7 und 8. (*I'm going on underground routes 7 and 8.*)

THE DATIVE WITH "ZU"

"**Zu**" means "*to*". When it is followed by "**der**" or "**dem**", the words are contracted to make "**zur**" and "**zum**":

Ich möchte **zum** Bahnhof. (*I'd like to go to the station.*)
Ich möchte **zur** Stadthalle. (*I'd like to go to the town hall.*)
Ich möchte **zum** Museum. (*I'd like to go to the museum.*)
Ich möchte **zu** den Thermen. (*I'd like to go to the baths.*)

"ZU" AND "IN"

German distinguishes between going <u>to</u> a place and going <u>into</u> it. You would tell the taxi driver to take you "**zum Museum**", because you want him to take you to it. But if you tell a friend that you are going to the museum, you are talking more about going inside. In that case, the German would be "**Ich gehe ins Museum**" (not "**zu**"). For more about this, see chapter 8, page 106.

THE DATIVE WITH "VON"

Here are some examples of the dative with "**von**" (*from, of*). When it is followed by "**dem**", the two words contract to "**vom**".

Ich komme **vom** Hermannplatz. (*I've come from Hermannplatz.*)
Ich komme **von** der Stadthalle. (*I've come from the town hall.*)
Ich komme **vom** Museum. (*I've come from the museum.*)
Ich komme **von** den Thermen. (*I've come from the baths.*)
But remember, when you say that you come from a country, instead of "**von**", you say "**aus**" (see page 17).

TWO VERBS IN A SENTENCE

You know that in a simple German sentence, the verb is always in the second position. If there are two verbs in a sentence, the second verb goes to the very end:

Wo **kann** man hier gut **essen**? (*Where can you get something good to eat?*)

Man **kann** hier gut **essen**. (*One/you can eat well here.*)

Ich **kann** das Hotel **empfehlen**. (*I can recommend the hotel.*)

Was **möchten** Sie **wissen**? (*What would you like to know?*)

GEHEN OR FAHREN

Both these German verbs mean "to go". "**Gehen**" usually implies going on foot and "**fahren**" usually means not on foot, but by car, bicycle, bus, train, etc.

COMMANDS

To tell someone to do something, reverse the positions of the verb and pronoun:

Gehen Sie nach rechts! (*Go right!*)

Fahren Sie mich bitte zum Museum! (*Drive me to the museum, please!*)

Entschuldigen Sie! (*Excuse me!*)

YOUR TURN

 1. DIRECTIONS (USING A MAP)

Charlottenburg, Berlin

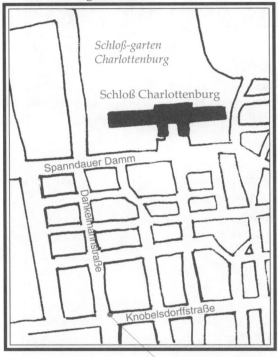

Schloß-garten Charlottenburg

Schloß Charlottenburg

Spanndauer Damm

Dankelmannstraße

Knobelsdorffstraße

You are here

A: Entschuldigung, ich suche das Schloß Charlottenburg.

B: Gehen sie hier ___ , die Dankelmannstraße ___ . Dann nach ___ in den Spanndauer Damm. Da ist ___ das Schloß Charlottenburg.

Check your answers with the key on page 99.

. FILL IN THE GAPS!

Tell the taxi driver where you want to go:

a) Ich möchte ___ Hotel.

b) Ich möchte ___ Museum.

c) Ich möchte ___ Brandenburger Tor.

d) Ich möchte ___ Bahnhof Zoo.

e) Ich möchte ___ Thermen.

f) Ich möchte ___ Kongresshalle.

g) Ich möchte ___ Schloß Charlottenburg.

h) Ich möchte ___ Rezeption.

Check your answers with the key on page 99.

3. DIRECTIONS

Fill in the gaps in the following conversation. You can check your answers with the key on page 99 and/or with the tape.

A: Entschuldigung! Wie kommen wir von hier ___

Hermannstraße?

B: Fahren Sie zuerst ___ Bus Nummer 10 bis ___ U-Bahn

Station, dann ___ U- Bahnlinie 3 bis ___ Kottbusser Tor und

dann ___ Kottbusser Tor ___ Linie 8 Richtung Leinestraße bis

___ Hermannstraße.

A: Vielen Dank!

. WO KANN MAN HIER . . . ?

Choose the right words from amongst the following, to make up five questions beginning with "**Wo kann man hier . . .**" that match the answers a – e.

anprobieren den Pullover Steak mit Salat trinken wohnen gut telefonieren essen ein Bier

a) In der Bar.

b) In der Umkleidekabine.

c) Am Bahnhof. Da ist ein Telefon.

d) Im Restaurant am Ufer.

e) Im Hotel Esplanade.

WORD LIST

die Bank (-en)	bank
der Bus (Busse)	bus
das Geld (-er)	money
die Halle (-n)	hall
die Information (-en)	information
die Kongresshalle	Congress building
die Linie (-n)	line, metro route
das Museum (Museen)	museum
der Platz (Plätze)	(town) square
die Rezeption (-en)	reception
die Richtung (-en)	direction
das Schloß (Schlösser)	palace, castle
das Souvenir (-s)	souvenir
die Stadthalle (-n)	town hall
die Station (-en)	station, stop
die Straße (-n)	street, road
das Taxi	taxi
die Thermen (=fem.plural)	baths, Turkish baths
der Tor (-e)	gate
die Touristenzentrale (-n)	tourist office
einkaufen	to go shopping
empfehlen	to recommend
entschuldigen	to excuse
können	to be able
stimmen	to be right
suchen	to look for, search
telefonieren	to telephone
umsteigen	to get out, change (trains, buses, etc)
warten	to wait
wechseln	to change
wissen	to know
also	so, thus
deutsch	German
erst	first
genau	exact, exactly
griechisch	Greek
italienisch	Italian
nach links	to the left
nach rechts	to the right
spanisch	Spanish
türkisch	Turkish
über	over
zu	to

KEY

1. DIRECTIONS (USING A MAP)
geradeaus
entlang
rechts
links

. FILL IN THE GAPS
a) zum Hotel; b) zum Museum; c) zum Brandenburger Tor;
d) zum Bahnhof Zoo; e) zu den Thermen; f) zur Kongresshalle;
g) zum Schloß Charlottenburg; h) zur Rezeption.

3. DIRECTIONS
zur Hermannstraße; mit dem Bus; zur U-Bahn Station; mit der
U-Bahnlinie; zum Kottbusser Tor; vom Kottbusser Tor; mit der Linie;
bis zum Hermannplatz.

. WO KANN MAN HIER . . . ?
a) Wo kann man hier ein Bier trinken?
b) Wo kann man hier den Pullover anprobieren?
c) Wo kann man hier telefonieren?
d) Wo kann man hier (gut) Steak mit Salat essen?
e) Wo kann man hier (gut) wohnen?

8 Arranging to meet

1. WANN TREFFEN WIR UNS?

Reception: Schott GmbH, Preußer. Guten Tag!
Schott GmbH, Preußer. Good morning/afternoon!

Waterman: Waterman. Guten Tag! Ich hätte gern mal mit Herrn Schott gesprochen.
Waterman. Good morning/afternoon! I would like to speak to Mr Schott.

Reception: Einen Moment, bitte. Ich verbinde.
One moment, please. I'm putting you through.

Waterman: Hallo! Hier ist John Waterman aus London. Wi geht es Ihnen?
Hello! This is John Waterman from London. How are you?

Schott: Gut, danke. Und Ihnen?
Fine, thank you. And you?

Waterman: Auch gut. Ich komme heute nachmittag um 5 Uhr in Berlin an. Wann können wir uns treffen
Also fine. I'm arriving in Berlin at 5 o'clock this afternoon. When could we meet?

Schott: Wie wär's mit heute abend?
How about this evening?

Waterman: Gut! Und wohin gehen wir? Gehen wir ins Restaurant oder treffen wir uns in einer Bar?
Fine! And where shall we go? Shall we go to a restaurant or meet in a bar?

Schott: Wie wär's mit dem Restaurant "Dicker Hund"? Da können wir gut reden.
How about the "Big Dog" restaurant? We can have a good talk there.

Waterman: Gute Idee! Und wann treffen wir uns da? So um halb acht?
Good idea! And when shall we meet? At about half past seven?

Schott: Gut! Dann bis heute abend.
Fine! I'll see you this evening.

1A. HOW IT SOUNDS

Ich hätte gern. Ich hätte gern mit Herrn Schott gesprochen. Ich hätte gern mal mit Herrn Schott gesprochen. Treffen. Wann können wir uns treffen? Wie wär's mit heute abend? Reden. Da können wir gut reden.

2. KOMMST DU HEUTE MIT INS KINO?

Ute: Berg.
Berg. [–answering telephone]

Anna: Hallo, Ute! Hier ist Anna. Kommst du heute mit ins Kino?
Hello, Ute! It's Anna. Are you coming to the cinema today?

Ute: Was gibt es denn?
What's on then?

Anna: "Das Geisterhaus".
"House of the Spirits".

Ute: Gut! Und wo treffen wir uns? Vor dem Kino?
Right! Where shall we meet? In front of the cinema?

Anna: Mhm. Das Kino findest du bestimmt nicht. Vielleicht besser im Cafe Einstein.
Mhm. I'm sure you won't find the cinema. Perhaps we'd better meet in the Cafe Einstein.

Ute: Da kann man aber nicht parken.
But you can't park there.

Anna: Oder am Brandenburger Tor?
Or at the Brandenburger Tor?

Ute: OK. Aber wo da? Unter dem Tor? Und um wieviel Uhr?
OK. But where exactly? Under the arch? And what time?

Anna: Unter dem Tor, so um halb sieben.
Under the arch, at about 6.30.

Ute: Gut! Bis dann! Tschüß!
Fine! See you soon! Bye!

Anna: Tschüß!

2A. HOW IT SOUNDS

Hallo, Ute! Hallo, Ute! Hier ist Anna. Kommst du mit? Kommst du mit ins Kino? Kommst du heute mit ins Kino? Vielleicht. Vielleicht besser im Cafe Einstein. Tschüß! Tschüß! Bis dann!

3. ICH HABE KEINE ZEIT

Petra: Meier.
Meier. [–answering telephone]

Stefan: Hallo, Petra! Hier ist Stefan. Kommst du heute abend mit ins Kino?
Hello, Petra! It's Stefan. Fancy coming to the cinema this evening?

Petra: Mhm, ins Kino? Was gibt es denn?
Mhm, to the cinema? What's on then?

Stefan: "Das Geisterhaus".
"House of the Spirits".

Petra: Nee. Ich habe keine Lust.
No. I don't fancy it.

Stefan: Kommst du dann mit in die Oper?
Would you like to come to the opera then?

Petra: Nein. Ich habe kein Geld.
No. I haven't any money.

Stefan: Oder gehst du mit essen?
Or would you like to go and have something to eat?

Petra: Tut mir leid, aber ich habe im Moment keinen
Hunger.
I'm sorry, but I'm not hungry at the moment.

Stefan: Hm. Keine Lust, kein Geld und keinen Hunger.
Dann gehe ich eben alleine. Hast du Probleme?
*Hm. No interest, no money, no hunger. Then I'll go
on my own. Is there something wrong?*

Petra: Nein. Ich habe keine Probleme. Tschüß!
No. There's nothing wrong. Bye!

Stefan: Tschüß!

3A. HOW IT SOUNDS

Keine Lust. Ich habe keine Lust. Kein Geld. Ich habe kein
Geld. Keinen Hunger. Ich habe keinen Hunger. Probleme. Ich
habe keine Probleme.

4. WIE WAR'S GESTERN?

Anna: Hallo, Stefan! Wie war's gestern mit Petra?
Wart ihr im Kino?
*Hello, Stefan! How did you get on with Petra
yesterday? Did you go to the cinema?*

Stefan: Nein. Petra hatte keine Lust.
No. Petra didn't fancy it.

Anna: Wart ihr essen?
Did you go and have something to eat?

Stefan: Nein, auch nicht. Petra hatte keinen Hunger.
No, not that either. Petra wasn't hungry.

Anna: Wart ihr in der Oper?
Did you go to the opera?

Stefan: Nein. Das war Petra zu teuer.
No. That was too expensive for Petra.

Anna: Wo wart ihr denn?
Where did you go then?

Stefan: Nirgends. Petra hatte zu nichts Lust. Ich glaube,
sie mag mich nicht.
*Nowhere. Petra didn't fancy anything. I think she
doesn't like me.*

4A. HOW IT SOUNDS

Wie war's gestern? Wie war's gestern im Kino? Wie war's gestern mit Petra im Kino? Petra hatte keine Lust. Petra hatte zu nichts Lust. Sie mag mich nicht. Ich glaube, sie mag mich nicht.

5. SIE SPRECHEN ABER GUT DEUTSCH!

Schott: Hallo, Herr Waterman!
Hello, Mr Waterman!

Waterman: Hallo, Herr Schott! Schön, Sie zu sehen!
Hello, Mr Schott! It's good to see you!

Schott: Ja. Es war mal wieder Zeit!
Yes. It was about time!

Waterman: Ja. Trinken wir einen Aperitif?
Yes. Shall we have an aperitif?

Schott: Mhm, ja. Einen Sherry.
Mhm, yes. A sherry.

Waterman: Trocken?
Dry?

Schott: Ja. Sie sprechen aber gut Deutsch, Herr Waterman.
Yes. You speak German really well, Mr Waterman.

Waterman: Ja, schon besser! Ich hatte in England einen Deutschkurs.
Better, yes! I did a German course in Engand.

Schott: Und möchten Sie weiterlernen?
And would you like to study it further?

Waterman: Ja, natürlich!
Yes, of course!

Schott: Na dann viel Glück und Prost auf Ihr Deutsch!
Well good luck then, and cheers to your German!

5A. HOW IT SOUNDS

Schön. Schön, Sie zu sehen! Es war Zeit. Es war mal wieder Zeit. Deutsch. Sie sprechen Deutsch. Sie sprechen aber gut Deutsch. Viel Glück! Viel Glück und Prost auf Ihr Deutsch!

INFORMATION

WHERE TO MEET

Of course, a town map will give you some idea of where you could meet up in a place you don't know. But if you want to find out about places where you can meet indoors, buy yourself a copy of a city magazine, like *Time Out* in Britain. In Berlin, for instance, you can buy *Tip* or *Zitty*. Here you will find out about restaurants or cafés or **Kneipen** where you could meet and be out of the rain!

BEING A GUEST AT SOMEONE'S HOME

Customs in Germany are very similar to in Britain. However, if you want to do everything right on a formal occasion, here are a few tips:

1. Flowers are always appreciated, even if 50 bouquets arrive at a big party!
2. Shaking hands is a normal way of greeting someone and of saying goodbye.
3. Don't try to squeeze your peas on the back of your fork. Germans turn their forks the other way up.
4. Leaving food on the plate is not a must, so do dig in!
5. Germans tend to leave their hands on the table rather than keeping them underneath it.
6. Even if it is only a semi-formal occasion like afternoon tea, you will rarely find Germans casually dressed.

So I raise my glass to you, after the host of course, and wish you much enjoyment in Germany and among the Germans.

LANGUAGE NOTES

WO? AND WOHIN?

Both words mean "where?" but there is a slight difference.

Wo sind Sie? means *Where are you?*
Wohin gehen Sie? means *Where are you going to?*

In "**wohin?**" there is an idea of movement.

"IN" WITH THE ACCUSATIVE

It was mentioned in chapter 7 (page 94) that, in German, "**in**"
is used to mean "*to*" when the sense is of "going <u>into</u>
something".

For instance, the answer to the question: "**Wohin gehen wir
heute abend?**" might be:

Wir gehen **in den** Park.
Wir gehen **in die** Kneipe.
Wir gehen **ins** Restaurant.
Wir gehen **in die** Discos von Berlin.

When there is a sense of movement into a place, "**in**" is
followed by the accusative case. "**In**" plus "**das**" contract to
"**ins**".

"IN" WITH THE DATIVE

Where there is no idea of movement into, and the person or
thing is <u>already in </u>the place described, "**in**" is followed by the
dative case. For instance, the answer to the question: "**Wo
treffen wir uns?**" (*Where are we meeting?*) might be:

Wir treffen uns **im** Park.
Wir treffen uns **in der** Kneipe.
Wir treffen uns **im** Restaurant.
Wir treffen uns **in den** Discos.

"**In**" plus "**dem**" contracts to "**im**".

OTHER WORDS LIKE "IN"

All the following words to do with place follow the same rule as "in":

an (*to*)
vor (*in front of*)
unter (*under*)
über (*over*)
zwischen (*between*)
auf (*on*)
neben (*near*)
hinter (*behind*)

KEIN PROBLEM!

"**Kein**" (*no*) is a negative article. It follows exactly the same pattern as "**ein**", changing its endings according to the case, but it also has a plural form:

	nominative	accusative	dative
masculine	**kein**	**keinen**	**keinem**
feminine	**keine**	**keine**	**keiner**
neuter	**kein**	**kein**	**keinem**
plural (all genders)	**keine**	**keine**	**keinen**

TALKING ABOUT THE PAST

If you want to continue learning German after you have finished this course, you will soon come across the past tense. As a taster, here are the past tenses of "**haben**" (*to have*) and "**sein**" (*to be*).

ich **hatte** kein Geld
Sie **hatten** eine Idee
du **hattest** eine Idee
er/sie/es **hatte** drei Bier

wir **hatten** keinen Hunger
Sie **hatten** einen Computer
ihr **hattet** ein Auto
sie **hatten** keine Lust

ich **war** allein
Sie **waren** in Deutschland
du **warst** in Deutschland
er/sie/es **war** zu teuer

wir **waren** im Kino
Sie **waren** verliebt
ihr **wart** pünktlich
sie **waren** in Hannover

YOUR TURN

1. WO IST MEIN SCHLÜSSEL?

Fill in the gaps in the conversation with the correct form of **"in"** plus the definite article. Then check your answers with the key on page 111 and/or the tape.

A: Wo ist mein Schlüssel?

B: Ist er ___ Restaurant?

Ist er ___ Kino?

Ist er ___ Tasche?

Ist er ___ U-Bahn?

A: Nein, da ist er nicht.

B: Oh, mein Gott!

2. WOHIN GEHEN WIR?

Fill in the gaps, as in exercise 1.

A: Wohin gehen wir heute abend?

B: ___ Kino?

___ Theater?

___ Oper?

___ Park?

A: Nein. Ich habe keine Lust.

3. QUESTIONS AND ANSWERS

Which of the answers, 1-6, goes with the following questions?

a) Kommst du mit ins Kino?

b) Wohin gehen wir heute abend?

c) Was trinken Sie?

d) Wo treffen wir uns?

e) Wo wart ihr?

f) Möchten Sie weiterlernen?

1) Ins Kino.
2) Nein. Ich habe keine Zeit.
3) Am Brandenburger Tor.
4) Ja, natürlich.
5) Einen Sherry.
6) Wir waren nirgends.

Check your answers with the key on page 111.

4. FILL IN THE GAPS!
Fill in the gaps in the following conversation, using these words:
war's war wart hatte wart hatte waren hatte
Then check your answers with the key on page 111 and /or the
tape.

Anna: Hallo, Stefan! Wie ___ gestern im Kino?

Stefan: Wir ___ nicht im Kino. Petra ___ keine Lust.

Anna: ___ ihr essen?

Stefan: Nein. Petra ___ keinen Hunger.

Anna: ___ ihr in der Oper?

Stefan: Nein. Das ___ Petra zu teuer. Sie ___ kein Geld.

Anna: Oh, mein Gott!

5. WHERE WAS THE MAN?
Listen to the conversation on the tape. Where was the man, and
where will he be going tomorrow? After listening to the tape,
check the key on page 111 to see how much you understood.

WORD LIST

der Aperitiv (-e)	aperitif
das Haus (Häuser)	house
der Hunger	hunger
das Kino (-s)	cinema
der Kurs (-e)	course
die Lust (Lüste)	pleasure, fancy
der Nachmittag (-e)	afternoon
die Oper (-n)	opera
der Sherry	sherry
parken	**to park**
reden	to talk, chat
sprechen	to speak
treffen	to meet
verbinden	to connect
allein	alone
bestimmt	certainly
gestern	yesterday
Nee	No (colloquial)
nirgends	nowhere
vielleicht	perhaps

USEFUL EXPRESSIONS

Es war mal wieder Zeit!	It was about time!
Ich habe keine Lust	I don't fancy it
Ich hätte gern mit . . . gesprochen	I would like to speak to . . .
Schön Sie zu sehen!	Good to see you!
Viel Glück!	Lots of luck!
Wann treffen wir uns?	When are we meeting?/shall we meet?
Wie war es (gestern)	How was it/How did you get on (yesterday)?
Wie wär es mit . . .	How about . . . ?

KEY

1. WO IST MEIN SCHLÜSSEL?
im Restaurant; im Kino; in der Tasche; in der U-Bahn.

2. WOHIN GEHEN WIR?
ins Kino; ins Theater; in die Oper; in den Park.

3. QUESTIONS AND ANSWERS
a 2; b 1; c 5; d 3; e 6; f 4.

4. FILL IN THE GAPS!
Wie war's gestern . . .; Wir waren nicht . . .; Petra hatte keine Lust;
Wart ihr essen?; Petra hatte keinen Hunger; Wart ihr in der Oper?;
Das war Petra zu teuer; Sie hatte kein Geld.

5. WHERE WAS THE MAN?
A: Müller.
B: Hallo Christian! Wo bist du denn?
A: Ich bin am Bahnhof in Berlin.
B: Oh, gut! Kannst du heute abend mit ins Kino?
A: Nein, heute habe ich Keine Zeit.
B: Und was machst du morgen?
A: Ich möchte chinesisch essen gehen. Kannst du mit?
B: Ja, gut, wo treffen wir uns?
A: Vorm "Mandarin". OK?
B: Gut, dann bis dann. Tschüß.
A: Tschüß.

Mini-Dictionary

ab away, from
Abend, der (–e) evening
abfahren to leave, depart
abholen to fetch
acht eight
achte eighth
Adresse, die (–n) address
Ahnung, die (–en) idea
   Keine Ahnung! No idea!
allein alone
alles all, everything
also so, thus
alt old
an to
anderer/e/es other
Angebot, im A. on offer
ankommen to arrive
anprobieren to try on
anrufen to call
Aperitiv, der (–e) aperitif
Apfel, der (Äpfel) apple
Apfelsaft, der (–säfte) apple juice
Apfelstrudel, der apple strudel
Apotheke, die (–n) chemist, pharmacy
April April
arbeiten to work
auch also
August August
aus out of, from
ausgebucht booked up
Bäckerei, die (–en) baker's

Bad, das (–er) bath
Bahn, die (–en) road, path, way
Bahnhof, der (–höfe) railway station
Bank, die (–en) bank
Bar, die (–s) bar
bei at (a place)
besser better
bestellen to order
bestimmt certainly
Bett, das (–en) bed
bezahlen to pay
Bier, das (–e) beer
billig cheap
Biologie, die biology
bis until
   Bis dann! See you soon!
bißchen, ein b. a little
bitte please; or "here you are" or "can I help you?"
blau blue
bleiben to stay
Bohne, die (–n) bean
Bratwurst, die (–würste) type of sausage
Briefmarke, die (–n) stamp
Brot, das (–e) bread
Brötchen, das bread roll
Buch, das (Bücher) book
Bus, der (Busse) bus
Champignon, der (–s) white mushroom
Chips, die (= plural) crisps

Computer, der (–s) computer
da there
danach afterwards
danke thank you
dann then
dein your
deutsch German
Deutschland Germany
Dienstag Tuesday
Disco, die (–s) disco
Donnerstag Thursday
Doppelzimmer, das (–) double room
Dose, die (–n) tin, can
drei three
dreißig thirty
dreizehn thirteen
dritte third
durchgebraten well-done (of meat)
Dusche, die (–n) shower
einfach simple, simply; single (ticket)
einkaufen to go shopping
eins one
Einzelzimmer, das (–) single room
Eis, das ice cream
elf eleven
elfte eleventh
empfehlen to recommend
englisch English; of meat: rare
entlang along
entschuldigen to excuse
Entschuldigung! Excuse me!
Erdnuß, die (–nüsse) peanut
erst first
essen to eat
Etage, die (–n) floor, storey
etwas something, somewhat
euer your
fahren to travel, to go
Fahrkarte, die (–n) ticket
Februar February
Film, der (–e) film
finden find
Flasche, die (–n) bottle
fliegen to fly
Flug, der (Flüge) flight
Forelle, die (–n) trout
Frau, die (–en) woman, wife

Frau Mrs
frei free
Freitag Friday
Fremdenverkehrsbüro, das (–s) tourist office
freuen to please
    Freut mich! Pleased to meet you!
früh early
Frühstück, das (–e) breakfast
fünf five
fünfte fifth
fünfzehn fifteen
fünfzig fifty
für for
Garage, die (–n) garage, parking
Gasthof, der (–höfe) restaurant
gebacken baked
geben to give
    Es gibt There is
    Gibt es? Is there?
gehen to go
    Es geht (mir gut) I'm fine
    Wie geht's? How are you?
Geld, das (–er) money
Gemüse, das vegetable
genau exact, exactly
geöffnet open(ed)
Gepäck, das (–e) luggage
geradeaus straight out
gern, ich hätte g. I would like
Geschäft, das (–e) shop
geschlossen shut, closed
geschmeckt, Hat es g.? Did you enjoy your meal?
gestern yesterday
Getränk, das (–e) drink
getrennt separated, separately
Glas, das (Gläser) glass
glauben to believe, to think
gleich immediately; same, alike
Gleis, das (–e) platform (railway)
Glück, das luck
glücklich happy
Gramm, das (–e) gramme
griechisch Greek
groß big, large
Größe, die (–n) size

grün green
gut good
Halbpension, die half board
Halle, die (–n) hall
Hand, die (Hände) hand
Hauptgericht, das (–e) main course
Haus, das (Häuser) house
Hauswein, der house wine
heiß hot
heißen to be called
hell light
Hering, der (–e) herring
Herr, der (–en) man, gentleman
Herr Mr
heute today
hier here
  hier unten under here
hin there
  hin und zurück there and back;
    return (ticket)
Hose, die (–n) pair of trousers
Hotel, das (–s) hotel
Huhn, das chicken
Hühnersuppe, die chicken soup
hundert one hundred
Hunger, der hunger
ihr her,its; their
Ihr your
in in
inclusive including
Information, die (–en) information
italienisch Italian
ja yes
Januar January
Juli July
Juni June
Kaffee, der (–s) coffee
kalt cold
Kännchen, das little pot
Karte, die (–n) menu
Kartoffel, die (–n) potato
Käse, der cheese
Kasten, der case, box
Katze, die (–n) cat
kaufen to buy
kein no
Keks, der (–e) biscuit

Kilo, das (–) kilogram
Kino, das (–s) cinema
klar clear
  Klar!, Alles klar! Fine!, Sure!
Klasse, die (–n) class
Kleid, das (–er) dress
klein small
Kneipe, die (–n) pub
kommen to come
Konferenz, die (–en) meeting
Konferenzraum, der (–räume)
  conference room
Kongresshalle, die (–n) Congress
  building
können to be able
Korridor, der (–e) corridor
kosten to cost
Kreditkarte, die (–n) credit card
Kuchen, der (–) cake
Kurs, der (–e) course
Kuß, der (Küsse) kiss
langsam slow, slowly
Leberwurst, die (–würste) liver sausage
lecker delicious
leid, Es tut mir l. I'm sorry
Lied, das (–er) song
Lift, der (–s or –e) lift
Linie, die (–n) line, metro route
links, nach links left
Liter, das (–) litre
Lust, die (Lüste) pleasure, fancy
  Lust haben zu to fancy
Mai May
Mann, der (Männer) man, husband
Mark, die (–) Mark
März March
Maschine, die (–n) machine, aeroplane
Massageraum, der (–räume) massage
  room
medium medium
mehr more
Mehrwertsteuer (MwSt), die (–n) VAT
mein my
Melone, die (–n) melon
Milch, die milk
Million, die million
Mineralwasser, das mineral water

Minute, die (–n) minute
mit with, by
mitkommen to accompany
Mittwoch Wednesday
möchte, ich m. I would like
Montag Monday
Morgen, der morning
Museum, das (Museen) museum
Mutter, die (Mütter) mother
nach after
Nachmittag, der (–e) afternoon
Nachspeise, die (–n) dessert
nächst next
Nacht, die (Nächte) night
Name, der (–n) name
Natürlich! Naturally!/Of course!
Nee! No! (colloquial)
nehmen to take
Nein! No!
neun nine
neunte ninth
nicht not
nichts nothing
nichts mehr nothing more
nirgends nowhere
noch still
November November
Nudel, die (–n) noodle
null zero, nought
Nummer, die (–n) number
nür only
Ober, Herr O.! Waiter! (to call him)
offen open
Oktober October
Öl, das oil
Oper, die (–n) opera
Orangensaft, der (–säfte) orange juice
Ort, der (–e) place
Ortszeit, die local time
Packung, die (–en) packet
Paprika, die (–) red, green or yellow pepper
parken to park
Parkplatz, der (–plätze) parking
passen to fit (of clothes)
Pension, die (–en) guest house
Person, die (–en) person

Pfennig, der (–e) German Pfennig (one–hundreth of a Mark)
Pizzaboden, der (–böden) pizza base
Platz, der (Plätze) place, seat; town square
Postkarte, die (–n) postcard
pro for, per
Problem, das (–e) problem
Prost! Cheers!
Pullover, der (–) pullover
Quatsch, der nonsense
Rechnung, die (–en) bill
rechts, nach rechts right, to the right
reden to talk, chat
Reis, der rice
Reise, die (–n) journey
reisen to travel
reservieren to reserve
Reservierung, die (–en) reservation
Rest, der (–e) rest
Restaurant, das (–s) restaurant
Rezeption, die (–en) reception
richtig correct
Richtung, die (–en) direction
rot red
Rumpsteak, das (–s) rump steak
sagen to say
Sahne, die cream
Salami, die (–s) salami
Salat, der (–e) salad/lettuce
Salzkartoffeln, die salt potatoes
Samstag Saturday
Sauce, die (–n) (*also* **Soße, die (–n)**) sauce
Sauna, die (–s) sauna
Schinken, der (–) ham
Schloß, das (Schlösser) palace, castle
Schlüssel, der (–) key
schmecken to taste
   Hat es geschmeckt? Did you enjoy your meal?
Schnitzel, das (–) fillet, cutlet
Scholle, die (–n) plaice
schön beautiful, lovely
   Schönen Abend! Have a good evening!
schreiben to write, spell

Wie schreibt man das? How do you spell that?

Schwarzwälderkirschtorte, die (–n) Black Forest gâteau

Schwimmbad, das (–er) swimming pool

schwimmen to swim

sechs six

sechste sixth

sehr very

sein his, its

sein to be

Sekunde, die (–n) second

Sherry, der sherry

September September

sieben seven

siebente seventh

siebzehn seventeenth

siebzig seventy

sofort straightaway

Sonnenbank, die (–e) solarium

Sonntag Sunday

sonst otherwise, else

Soße, die (–n) (*also* **Sauce, die (–n)**) sauce

Souvenier, das (–s) souvenir

spanisch Spanish

spät late

Wie spät ist es? What time is it?

Speisekarte, die (–n) menu

Speisewagen, der (–) restaurant car

sprechen to speak

Stadt, die (Städte) town, city

Stadthalle, die (–n) town hall

Station, die (–en) station, stop

Steak, das (–s) steak

stimmen to be right

Stimmt das? Is that right?

Stimmt so. Keep the change.

Stop, der stop

Straße, die (–n) street, road

studieren to study

Stunde, die (–n) hour

suchen to look for, search

Supermarkt, der (–märkte) supermarket

Suppe, die (–n) soup

süß sweet

T–shirt, das (–s) T–shirt

Tag, der (–e) day

Tasse, die (–n) cup

Taxi, das (–s) taxi

Tee, der (–s) tea

Teewurst, die (–würste) type of sausage

Telefon, das (–s) telephone

telefonieren to telephone

Telefonnummer, die (–n) telephone number

teuer expensive

Theater, der (–) theatre

Thermen, die baths, Turkish baths

Tisch, der (–e) table

Toilette (–n) toilet

Tomate, die (–n) tomato

Tomatensuppe, die (–n) tomato soup

Ton, der (Töne) beep, tone, sound

Tor, der (–e) gate

total completely

Touristenzentrale, die (–n) tourist office

treffen to meet

trinken to drink

trocken dry

Tschüß! Bye!

türkisch Turkish

Tüte, die (–n) plastic bag

über over

übrigens besides, by the way

Uhr, die (–en) hour

Um wieviel Uhr? At what time?

um around, at

Umkleidekabine, die (–n) changing room

umsteigen to get out, change (trains, buses, etc)

ungefähr about, roughly

unser our

Vater, der (Väter) father

verbinden to connect

verliebt in love

Verspätung, die (–n) delay

verstehen to understand

vielleicht perhaps

vier four
vierte fourth
Vollpension, die full board
vor before, in front of
Vorspeise, die (–n) starter
vorzüglich excellent
Wagen, der (–) carriage (train)
warten to wait
warum? why?
was? what?
WC, das (–s), Toilette, die (–n) toilet
wechseln to change
Wein, der (–e) wine
weiß white
wer? who?
Whisky, der whisky
wichtig important
wie? how?
    Wie bitte? Pardon? (you did not hear)
    Wie geht's? How are you?
    Wie wär es? How about?
wieder again
Wiederhören, Auf W.! Goodbye! (on telephone)
Wiedersehen, Auf W.! Goodbye!
wieviel? how many?

wirklich really, truly
wissen to know
wo? where?
Woche, die (–n) week
woher? where from?
wohnen to live
wunderbar wonderful,lovely
Wurst (Würste), die sausage
zehn ten
zehnte tenth
Zeit, die time
    Es war mal wieder Zeit! It was about time!
Zeitansage, die speaking clock
Zigarette, die (–n) cigarette
Zimmer, das (–) room
zu to
zuerst first (of all)
Zug, der (Züge) train
Zum Wohl! Good health!
zurück back, back again
zusammen together
zwanzig twenty
zwei two
zweimal twice
zweite second
Zwiebel, die (–n) onion
zwölf twelve

ENGLISH-GERMAN

able, to be a. können
    I am a., I can ich kann
about, roughly ungefähr
accompany, to mitkommen
address Adresse, die (–n)
aeroplane Flugzeug, das; Maschine, die (–n)
after nach
afternoon Nachmittag, der (–e)
    Good afternoon! Guten Tag!
afterwards danach
again wieder
all alles
    That's all Das ist alles
alone allein
along entlang

    along the road die Straße entlang
also auch
another noch ein(e)
aperitif Aperitiv, der (–e)
apple strudel Apfelstrudel, der
apple Apfel, der (Äpfel)
apple juice Apfelsaft, der (–säfte)
April April
around um
arrive, to ankommen
at um (time), bei (place)
August August
away ab
back (again) zurück
bag (plastic) Tüte, die (–n)
bake, to backen

baked gebacken
baker's Bäckerei, die (–en)
bank Bank, die (–en)
bar Bar, die (–s)
bath Bad, das (–er)
  to have a bath ein Bad nehmen
baths, Turkish Thermen, die
be, to sein
  I am ich bin
bean Bohne, die (–n)
beautiful schön
bed Bett, das (–en)
beer Bier, das (–e)
before vor, vorher
believe, to glauben
better besser
big groß
bill Rechnung, die (–en)
biology Biologie, die
biscuit Keks, der (–e)
black schwarz
blue blau
board, full Vollpension, die
  half Halbpension, die
book Buch, das (Bücher)
book, to reservieren
booked up ausgebucht
bottle Flasche, die (–n)
bread Brot, das (–e)
breakfast Frühstück, das (–e)
brown braun
bus Bus, der (Busse)
buy, to kaufen
cake Kuchen, der (–)
call anrufen
called, to be c. heißen
  I am called ich heiße
can (I can etc) See "able"
carriage (train) Wagen, der (–)
castle Schloß, das (Schlösser)
cat Katze, die (–n)
certain(ly) sicher, bestimmt
change, to wechseln; (trains, etc)
  umsteigen
changing room Umkleidekabine, die
  (–n)
cheap billig

Cheers! Prost!
cheese Käse, der
chemist's Apotheke, die (–n)
chicken Huhn, das
chicken soup Hühnersuppe, die
cigarette Zigarette, die (–n)
cinema Kino, das (–s)
city Stadt, die (Städte)
class Klasse, die (–n)
coffee Kaffee, der (–s)
cold kalt
come, to kommen, ankommen
completely total
computer Computer, der (–s)
conference Konferenz, die (–en)
conference room Konferenzraum, der
  (–räume)
connect, to verbinden
correct richtig
corridor Korridor, der (–e)
cost, to kosten
  What does ... cost? Wieviel kostet..?
  Was kostet ...?
course Kurs, der (–e)
course, Of c.! Natürlich!,
  Selbstverständlich!
cream Sahne, die
credit card Kreditkarte, die (–n)
  Can I pay by c.c.? Kann ich mit
  Kreditkarte bezahlen?
crisps Chips, die (plural)
cup Tasse, die (–n)
dark dunkel
day Tag, der (–e)
December Dezember
delay Verspätung, die (–n)
delicious lecker
depart, to abfahren
dessert Nachspeise, die (–n)
direction Richtung, die (–en)
disco Disco, die (–s)
dog Hund, der (–e)
double room Doppelzimmer, das (–)
dress Kleid, das (–er)
drink, to trinken
drink Getränk, das (–e)
dry trocken

early früh
eat essen
eight acht
eighth achte
eleven elf
eleventh elfte
else, Something e.? Sonst noch etwas?
evening Abend, der (–e)
    Good evening! Good evening!
    Have a good evening! Schönen
    Abend!
everything alles
exact(ly) genau
excellent vorzüglich
excuse, to entschuldigen
    Excuse me! Entschuldigung!,
    Entschuldigen Sie!
expensive teuer
fancy, to Lust haben
    I don't fancy (it) Ich habe keine Lust
    (dazu)
father Vater, der (Väter)
February Februar
fetch, to abholen
fifth fünfte
fifty fünfzig
film Film, der (–e)
find, to finden
first, first of all erst, zuerst
fit, to (clothes) passen
five fünf
flight Flug, der (Flüge)
floor Fußboden, der
floor (storey) Etage, die (–n)
fly, to fliegen
for für
for (per) pro
four vier
fourth vierte
free frei
Friday Freitag
from von, (a country) aus
full voll
garage Garage, die (–n)
gate Tor, der (–e)
gateau Torte, die (–n)
gentleman Herr, der (–en)

German deutsch
Germany Deutschland
glass Glas, das (Gläser)
good gut
Goodbye! Auf Wiedersehen!, (on the
    phone) Auf Wiederhören!
Good health! Zum Wohl!
gramme Gramm, das (–e)
Greek griechisch
green grün
guest house Pension, die (–en)
hall Halle, die (–n)
ham Schinken, der
hand Hand, die (Hände)
happy glücklich
Hello! Hallo!
her ihr
here hier
herring Hering, der (–e)
his sein
hot heiß
hotel Hotel, das (–s)
hour Stunde, die (–n), Uhr, die (–en)
house Haus, das (Häuser)
house wine Hauswein, der
how? wie?
    How about? Wie wär es?
    How are you? Wie geht's?, Wie geht
    es Ihnen?
how many? wieviel?
hunger Hunger, der
husband Mann, der (Männer)
ice cream Eis, das
idea Ahnung, die (–en), Idee, die (–n)
    Good idea! Gute Idee!
    No idea! Keine Ahnung!
immediately gleich
important wichtig
in in
including inclusive
information Information, die (–en)
Italian italienisch
January Januar
July Juli
June Juni
journey Reise, die (–n)
    Have a good journey! Gute Reise!

key Schlüssel, der
kilogram Kilo, das (–)
kiss Kuß, der (Küsse)
kiss, to küssen
know, to wissen (a fact), kennen (a person)
   I don't know Ich weiß nicht
late spät
leave, to lassen, (depart) abfahren
left, to the left links, nach links
lift Lift, der (–s or –e)
light (pale) hell
like, I would l. ich hätte gern, ich möchte
line Linie, die (–n)
litre Liter, das (–n)
little klein
   a little ein bißchen
look for, to suchen
love, to lieben
love, in l. verliebt
lovely schön
luggage Gepäck, das (–e)
machine Maschine, die (–n)
main course Hauptgericht, das (–e)
man Mann, der (Männer)
March März
Mark Mark, die (–)
May Mai
meet, to treffen
meeting Konferenz, die (–en)
melon Melone, die (–n)
menu Speisekarte, die (–n), Karte, die (–n)
milk Milch, die
million Million, die (–en)
mine mein
mineral water Mineralwasser, das
minute Minute, die (–n)
moment, One m. please Moment, bitte
Monday Montag
money Geld, das (–er)
more mehr
morning Morgen
   Good morning! Guten Morgen!, Guten Tag!
mother Mutter, die (Mütter)

Mr Herr
Mrs Frau
museum Museum, das (Museen)
my mein
name Name, der (–n)
   What is your name? Wie ist Ihr Name?
next nächst
night Nacht, die (Nächte)
nine neun
ninety neunzig
ninth neunte
no kein
No! Nein!, (colloquial) Nee!
nonsense Quatsch, der
noodle Nudel, die (–n)
nothing nichts
   nothing more nichts mehr
nought null
November November
nowhere nirgends
number Nummer, die (–n)
October Oktober
oil Öl, das
old alt
once einmal
one ein, eins
onion Zwiebel, die (–n)
only nür
open(ed) offen, geöffnet
opera Oper, die (–n)
orange juice Orangensaft, der (–säfte)
order, to bestellen
other anderer/e/es
otherwise sonst
our unser
out (of) aus
over über
packet Packung, die (–en)
palace Schloß, das (Schlösser)
park, to parken
parking Parkplatz, der (–plätze)
pay, to bezahlen
peanut Erdnuß, die (–nüsse)
pepper Pfeffer, der/ Paprika, die (–)
per pro
perhaps vielleicht

person Person, die (–en)
pizza base Pizzaboden, der
place Ort, der (–e); (seat) Platz, der (Plätze)
plaice Scholle, die (–n)
platform (railway) Gleis, das (–e)
please, to freuen
please bitte
postcard Postkarte, die (–n)
potato Kartoffel, die (–n)
prefer, I would p. Ich möchte lieber
problem Problem, das (–e)
pub Kneipe, die (–n)
pullover Pullover, der
railway station Bahnhof, der (–höfe)
really wirklich
reception Rezeption, die (–en)
recommend, to empfehlen
red rot
repeat, to wiederholen
   Can you repeat that, please Noch einmal, bitte
reservation Reservierung, die (–en)
reserve, to reservieren
rest Rest, der (–e)
restaurant Restaurant, das (–s), Gasthof, der (–höfe)
restaurant car Speisewagen, der (–)
rice Reis, der
right, to the right rechts, nach rechts
right (correct) richtig
right, to be r. stimmen
   That's right Das stimmt
road Bahn, die (–en), Straße, die (–n)
roll (bread) Brötchen, das
room das Zimmer
salad Salat, der
salt Salz, das
Saturday Samstag
sauce Sauce, die or Soße, die
sauna Sauna, die (–s)
sausage Wurst (Würste), die
say, to sagen
second zweite
second Sekunde, die (–n)
separate(ly) getrennt
September September

seven sieben
seventh siebente
sherry Sherry, der
shop Geschäft, das (–e)
shopping, to go s. einkaufen
shower Dusche, die (–n)
shut, to schliessen
shut, closed geschlossen
sign, to unterschreiben
simple, simply einfach
single (ticket) einfach
   Single or return? Einfach oder hin und zurück?
single room Einzelzimmer, das (–)
six sechs
sixth sechste
size Größe, die (–n)
slow, slowly langsam
small klein
so, therefore denn, darum
so, thus also
solarium Sonnenbank, die (–e)
something, somewhat etwas
song Lied, das (–er)
sorry, I'm s. Es tut mir leid
soup Suppe, die (–n)
souvenir Souvenier, das (–s)
Spanish spanisch
speak sprechen
speaking clock Zeitansage, die
spell, to schreiben
   How do you spell that? Wie schreibt man das?
square (town) Platz, der (Plätze)
stamp Briefmarke, die (–n)
starter Vorspeise, die (–n)
station, stop Station, die (–en)
stay, to bleiben
steak Steak, das (–s)
still noch
storey Etage, die (–n)
straight on geradeaus
straightaway sofort, gleich
street Straße, die (–n)
study, to studieren
Sunday Sonntag
supermarket Supermarkt, der (–märkte)

sweet süß
swim, to schwimmen
swimming pool Schwimmbad, das (–er)
T–shirt T–shirt, das (–s)
table Tisch, der (–e)
take, to nehmen
talk, chat, to reden
taste, to schmecken
taxi Taxi, das (–)
tea Tee, der (–s)
telephone Telefon, das (–s)
telephone number Telefonnummer
telephone, to telefonieren, anrufen
ten zehn
tenth zehnte
thank you danke
theatre Theater, der (–)
their ihr
then dann
there (over there) da, (to there) hin
there is es gibt
think, to denken, glauben
third dritte
thirty dreißig
three drei
Thursday Donnerstag
ticket (travel) Fahrkarte, die (–n)
time Zeit, die
   What is the time? Wie spät ist es?
   At what time! Um wieviel Uhr?
time, local t. Ortszeit, die
tin Dose, die (–n)
to an, zu
today heute
together zusammen
toilet WC, das
tomato Tomate, die (–n)
tomato soup Tomatensuppe, die (–n)
tomorrow morgen
tourist office Touristenzentrale, die
      (–n),
   Fremdenverkehrsbüro, das (–s)
town Stadt, die (Städte)
town hall Stadthalle, die (–n)

train Zug, der (Züge)
travel, to fahren, reisen
trousers, pair of t. Hose, die (–n)
trout Forelle, die (–n)
try on, to (clothes) anprobieren
Tuesday Dienstag
Turkish türkisch
twelfth zwölfte
twelve zwölf
twenty zwanzig
twice zweimal
two zwei
under unter
understand, to verstehen
until bis
VAT Mehrwertsteuer (MwSt), die (–n)
vegetable Gemüse, das
very sehr
wait, to warten
Waiter! (to call him) Herr Ober!
warm warm
Wednesday Mittwoch
week Woche, die (–n)
well wohl
   I'm well Es geht mir gut
what? was?
where? wo?
where from? woher?
whisky Whisky, der
white weiß
who? wer?
why? warum?
wine Wein, der (–e)
with mit
woman Frau, die (–en)
wonderful wunderbar
work, to arbeiten
write, to schreiben
yellow gelb
yes ja
yesterday gestern
your dein (inf. sing.), euer (inf. plural),
   Ihr

Index